Towards Nuclear Zero

David Cortright and Raimo Väyrynen

Towards Nuclear Zero

David Cortright and Raimo Väyrynen

IISS The International Institute for Strategic Studies

The International Institute for Strategic Studies

Arundel House I 13–15 Arundel Street I Temple Place I London I WC2R 3DX I UK

First published April 2010 by **Routledge**
4 Park Square, Milton Park, Abingdon, Oxon, OX14 4RN

for **The International Institute for Strategic Studies**
Arundel House, 13–15 Arundel Street, Temple Place, London, WC2R 3DX, UK
www.iiss.org

Simultaneously published in the USA and Canada by **Routledge**
270 Madison Ave., New York, NY 10016

Routledge is an imprint of Taylor & Francis, an Informa Business

DIRECTOR-GENERAL AND CHIEF EXECUTIVE John Chipman
EDITOR Tim Huxley
MANAGER FOR EDITORIAL SERVICES Ayse Abdullah
ASSISTANT EDITOR Janis Lee
COVER/PRODUCTION John Buck

The International Institute for Strategic Studies is an independent centre for research, information and debate on the problems of conflict, however caused, that have, or potentially have, an important military content. The Council and Staff of the Institute are international and its membership is drawn from almost 100 countries. The Institute is independent and it alone decides what activities to conduct. It owes no allegiance to any government, any group of governments or any political or other organisation. The IISS stresses rigorous research with a forward-looking policy orientation and places particular emphasis on bringing new perspectives to the strategic debate.

The Institute's publications are designed to meet the needs of a wider audience than its own membership and are available on subscription, by mail order and in good bookshops. Further details at www.iiss.org.

Printed and bound in Great Britain by Bell & Bain Ltd, Thornliebank, Glasgow

British Library Cataloguing in Publication Data
A catalogue record for this book is available from the British Library

Library of Congress Cataloging in Publication Data

ISBN 978-0-415-59528-5
ISSN 0567-932X

ADELPHI 410

Contents

ACKNOWLEDGEMENTS

We owe gratitude to many people who contributed to the writing of this book. We benefitted most from the support of Eliot Fackler, research assistant at the Kroc Institute for International Peace Studies at the University of Notre Dame, who provided help with virtually every aspect of the book's preparation. He participated in our writing sessions, maintained control of evolving chapter documents, researched and fact-checked dozens of sources, and helped with citations and text editing. His meticulous professionalism shaped nearly every page of this volume. We also received important assistance from Jennifer Glick, publications director at the Fourth Freedom Forum, who assisted with editing, the preparation of citations and the verification of sources.

The book reflects valuable insights gleaned from the conference, 'The NPT and a World without Nuclear Weapons,' cosponsored by the Finnish Institute of International Affairs and the Kroc Institute for International Peace Studies, which took place in Helsinki 22–24 October 2009. Most significant were the keynote addresses of Margaret Beckett, Gareth Evans and William Perry, which shaped the conference and influenced our thinking as we crafted this volume. We gained important research findings and policy analyses from commissioned papers written by Rebecca Johnson, Harald Müller, T.V. Paul, and George Perkovich. We also benefitted from papers submitted by Ian Biggs, Tarja Cronberg, James Goodby, Mohammad Shaker, Sverre Lodgaard and Henrik Salander.

We received assistance from Alistair Millar, Etel Solingen, William Potter, Jonathan Schell, Avner Cohen, and Harald Müller, who either read and commented on portions of the manuscript or answered queries about sources and specific points of fact and analysis. We benefitted most from very extensive comments and queries from Mark Fitzpatrick, director of the non-proliferation and disarmament programme at the International Institute for Strategic Studies in London, and from Tim Huxley, senior editor of the Adelphi series, also at IISS. We are grateful for support in preparing the manuscript from Janis Lee, assistant editor for the Adelphis at IISS.

We are most grateful to our respective institutes, the Finnish Institute of International Affairs and the Kroc Institute for International Peace Studies at the University of Notre Dame, for their co-sponsorship of the Helsinki conference and support for our efforts in researching and writing this volume. Although we benefitted from many in preparing this volume, we take full responsibility for the analyses presented here and for any errors of fact or interpretation that may exist in the volume.

PREFACE

Rarely in the atomic age have hopes been raised as high as they are now for genuine progress towards disarmament. The new receptivity to nuclear abolition is reflected in the policy declarations of the Obama administration and other governments, and was sparked by a wave of private initiatives that started in 2007 led by former US Secretary of State George Shultz and other former senior officials and political leaders in many countries. Yet despite the glowing pledges of support for a world without nuclear weapons, questions arise about the sincerity of the nuclear-weapons states. They vow to get rid of these weapons at Nuclear Non-proliferation Treaty (NPT) Review Conferences and international summit meetings, yet in their national security policies they cling to the bomb and show no sign of abandoning nuclear deterrence policies. The new US-Russia strategic reduction treaty lowers ceilings for deployed nuclear warheads by more than 30%, but the number of readily useable weapons will decline very little.[1] A broad consensus exists on the urgency of stemming proliferation, yet little progress is visible in attempts at persuading North Korea and Iran to abandon nuclear capability or in reducing nuclear dangers in South Asia. Russia and the West affirm their common commitment to security cooperation, yet they differ on a broad range of issues and have lost much of the spirit of partnership that flourished briefly in the immediate post-Cold War years. A critical juncture may be approaching. If the soaring rhetoric of disarmament can not produce more substatntial policy results, efforts to build support for nuclear abolition could collapse into cynicism, and an opportunity may be missed to advance international security.

Officials who cling to nuclear weapons are reluctant to part with policies they consider vital to security. Nuclear deterrence has kept the peace, they claim, and must be preserved to prevent world war. Security concerns are the fundamental justification for maintaining reliance on nuclear weapons. They are also principal reasons why proliferating states seek to acquire these weapons, to guard against perceived security threats and enhance national power and status. Yet empirical evidence and case studies cast doubt on these justifications. Nuclear deterrence was not the only factor preventing war between the major powers. It has not stopped wars and armed conflicts in other states. It cannot prevent or deter global terrorist threats. The presumed link between extended deterrence and non-proliferation is not confirmed in quantitative studies. Great-power adherence to nuclear weapons validates these weapons for others. The continued divide between nuclear haves and have-nots impedes non-proliferation cooperation and threatens the NPT regime.

The security argument can be turned around: nations are safer and more secure without the bomb. Dozens of governments have made that determination in giving up nuclear-weapons programmes. Countering the threat of proliferation requires a commitment to disarmament. A strategy of progressive denuclearisation can enhance security and is fully compatible with political realism. Deterrence and the balancing of power do not disappear as nations reduce nuclear dependency. Deterrence continues in new forms even in a world without nuclear weapons as nations rely on the knowledge and capability to reconstitute weapons as a hedge against cheating.

This book examines the challenges and opportunities associated with achieving a world without nuclear weapons. It is inspired by the conference, 'The Nonproliferation Treaty and a World Without Nuclear Weapons', held in Helsinki, Finland, 22–24 October 2009, co-sponsored by the Finnish Institute of International Affairs and the Kroc Institute for International Peace Studies at the University of Notre Dame. At the conference former US Defense Secretary William Perry, former British Foreign Secretary Margaret Beckett, and former Australian Foreign Secretary Gareth Evans joined dozens of other experts and former officials from many countries to examine the complex issues and dilemmas associated with ending reliance on nuclear weapons. This volume is not a record of the conference proceedings but a synthesis of participants' insights and an expression of our own analyses and perspectives. We intend these pages as a contribution to a more informed and realistic assessment of achieving security without nuclear weapons.

CHAPTER ONE

Why Disarmament? Why Now?

Calls for nuclear disarmament are as old as the nuclear age. The awesome, destructive power unleashed on the cities of Hiroshima and Nagasaki in 1945 prompted immediate political plans to put the weapon under international control and prevent its use again, with atomic energy confined solely to peaceful purposes. The United States and the Soviet Union were unable to agree, however, as the competition for power in the post-war world and a lack of mutual trust stood in the way of disarmament.

The very first resolution of the newly created United Nations (UN) in January 1946 called for the creation of an Atomic Energy Commission to develop proposals 'for the elimination from national arsenals of atomic weapons and of all other major weapons adaptable to mass destruction'.[1] This was followed a few months later by the US government's Baruch Plan, which called for the establishment of an international body that would inspect and assure the dismantlement of nuclear-weapons facilities in all countries, and impose sanctions, including military means, against offending nations, with the dismantling of existing weapons (in essence a US atomic monopoly) at the conclusion of the process. The Baruch Plan was preceded by the Acheson–Lilienthal Report, which stressed the need for what today would be called full-scope safeguards against the military use of atomic energy and the global control of the nuclear fuel cycle. The Soviet Union rejected the Baruch Plan because it did not have confidence in the US promise to abolish its nuclear weapons. Moscow wanted to keep its options open and retain its veto in nuclear matters.[2]

In 1961 the US and Soviet governments issued the 'Joint Statement of Agreed Principles for Disarmament Negotiations' at the United Nations, also known as the McCloy–Zorin plan. It was an ambitious proposal that called for the elimination of all weapons of mass destruction in three successive phases. The proposal led to the creation of an 18-member UN committee on disarmament (ENDC), and the submission of differing draft treaties by the two sides, but no progress was achieved in negotiating disarmament. The Treaty on the Non-Proliferation of Nuclear Weapons (Nuclear Non-Proliferation Treaty, or NPT) in 1968 retained an echo of the previous disarmament commitments in its Article VI provisions for negotiations on disarmament but otherwise was an imperfect effort to establish peaceful control of nuclear energy and stem the spread of nuclear weapons.

By the 1970s, attempts to promote nuclear abolition had run into sand and were replaced by agreements to control and stabilise the US–Soviet nuclear arms race, which had reached alarming levels both qualitatively and quantitatively. The 'second Cold War' from 1978 to 1985 placed even these limited agreements in jeopardy. It was a sign of the times that the most radical demands by the peace movement focused on freezing the strategic arms race and eliminating nuclear weapons only from 'Poland to Portugal'.

A major political turning point occurred in January 1986 when Mikhail Gorbachev outlined a three-phase programme of nuclear disarmament by the year 2000 under effective international control.[3] Although Washington rejected the Soviet proposal, a new atmosphere of cooperation emerged which carried over to the Reykjavik Summit later that year, where Gorbachev and Ronald Reagan engaged in serious discussions on the abolition of nuclear weapons.

The call for the elimination of nuclear weapons has gained political urgency in recent years. The new attention to disarmament reflects fundamental changes in the military and political roles of nuclear weapons as a result of transformations in the international order. The present advocacy of nuclear abolition stems in part from the recognition that international power relations are changing inexorably. Shifting power alignments and the spread of nuclear weapons are eroding the effectiveness of deterrence and the old bipolar international order centred on Russia and the United States. These trends have important implications for the new international discourse on the necessity and possibility of eliminating nuclear weapons.

Multipolarity

The proliferation of nuclear weapons alters the traditional international power structure and creates growing political uncertainty. Nuclear deterrence was complicated but still manageable in a world with two or three great powers. As the number of nuclear-armed states increases, it becomes harder to estimate states' capabilities and intentions, and the possibility of error increases. Coalition-building opportunities increase, and the risk of unstable political alignments grows. The danger of terrorist acquisition threatens the very nature of state power, with weapons of ultimate destruction potentially in the hands of non-state actors.

The rise of new nuclear powers creates a flawed multipolar system in which objective measures of power and influence apply only imperfectly. Smaller and weaker countries that would otherwise have to comply with the demands of the major powers can resist these pressures by acquiring nuclear weapons, although often at a price of damage inflicted on their economies by external punishments. Analysts have written of the phenomenon of 'small state deterrence' in which a state would need only a small number of weapons and rudimentary means of delivery to dissuade a major power from invading or attacking.[4] The traditional rules of the balance of conventional military power do not apply in an international system with multiple nuclear-weapons states. A few dozen nuclear devices, or even fewer, would help a state to equalise the balance of destruction in an otherwise asymmetric system of states. In the nuclear age the balance of terror alters the balance of power.

The proliferation of nuclear weapons is both a cause and consequence of the growing decentralisation and multipolarity of international relations. The acquisition of nuclear weapons by new states creates more centres with 'unit veto', to use Morton Kaplan's term.[5] The proliferation of nuclear weapons poses a challenge to traditional power balancing, which is based on economic and other factors in addition to military resources.

The acquisition of nuclear capability is often a goal of 'desperate' countries (Iran, Pakistan, North Korea) seeking to equalise asymmetric power relations. 'Desperate' countries are not 'failed' states but regimes that feel the need to improve their relative standing internationally and domestically by the short-cut of possessing weapons of mass destruction (WMD). These regimes perceive their position as inferior to other powers and uncertain in the domestic context. Nuclear acquisition is a means to prop up the regime at home and abroad.

Deterrence diluted

The proliferation challenges of the post-Cold War era are changing the role of nuclear weapons and the nature of deterrence. In the past, deterrence was primarily bilateral in nature, and the East–West security relationship was organised around structural bipolarity and nuclear deterrence. In this context, the US–Soviet relationship naturally loomed largest, but incipient deterrence relationships also emerged between these powers and China, between India and China, and later between India and Pakistan. The primitive deterrence relationship between France and the Soviet Union had implications for the security position of West Germany.

Deterrence relationships among countries now appear to be built on triads rather than bilateral relations. In what is referred to as the 'first nuclear era', the dominant triad was the United States, the USSR and China. Today, China, India and Pakistan form another, Asian triangle of nuclear deterrence.[6] In the future, yet another triad might emerge in the Middle East: Israel, Iran and Syria. A simple property of triangles is that they permit coalitions of two against one when new types of nuclear alliances emerge. As triangles start interacting in the second or even third nuclear eras, deterrence relationships will become more complex and difficult to manage.

In a multipolar international system deterrence has to be 'shared' among more targets, which tends to dilute its political effectiveness. Indian political scientist T.V. Paul speaks in this context about 'complex deterrence', which is ambiguous and structurally indeterminate, sending unclear and mixed signals to and from the relevant actors.[7] The rise of new nuclear weapons states increases the unpredictability of international relations and deterrence. This trend is reinforced by concerns that terrorists might obtain and use these weapons, although that threat has often been exaggerated.[8]

A reason for the United States and other major powers to advocate the abolition of nuclear weapons is to address these challenges to the effectiveness of deterrence. This is acknowledged in the article 'A World Free From Nuclear Weapons', which was submitted to the Wall Street Journal in January 2007. Written former US secretaries of state George Shultz and Henry Kissinger, former US Defense Secretary William Perry and former Senator Sam Nunn (often collectively referred to as the Hoover Institution group, after the public policy think tank of which they are members), it declared: 'It is far from certain that we can successfully replicate the old Soviet-America "mutually assured destruction" (MAD) with an increasing number of potential nuclear enemies world-wide without dramatically increasing the risk that nuclear weapons will be used'.[9]

MAD still prevails in strategic relations between Russia and the United States, but it has been sinking rather deep in the sediment of their mutual relations. If deterrence fails, the use of nuclear weapons, even first use, is still the official doctrine, although this threat has lost much of its credibility. During the Georgian crisis in August 2008 neither the US nor Russia made reference to nuclear weapons.

The international order based on nuclear deterrence and the potential use of nuclear weapons contradicts the principles of political realism. The employment of nuclear weapons would not achieve political gain in the traditional Clausewitzian understanding of the utility of military force. Rather it would be an unmitigated disaster that would significantly reduce the international standing of the perpetrator. If nuclear weapons-states aim to increase their relative power, as realists argue, why would they deliberately destroy the basis of that power?[10]

The dilution of nuclear deterrence leads to the search for alternative sources of power and influence over international affairs. The cost/benefit ratio of nuclear weapons is tilting in the direction of growing risks and liabilities. Somewhat para-doxically, the major states may gain in power and security by reducing the global emphasis on nuclear weapons and finding alternative solutions to security problems. The United States can gain from its strong comparative advantage in conventional military technologies, and, as Barry Posen has suggested, from its control of the global commons.[11]

Nuclear realism

Historically, discussions of nuclear disarmament have had a utopian quality. Advocates and opponents alike tend to view disarmament as an absolute condition, an end point beyond which the realities of politics and security no longer seem to apply. The concept of nuclear abolition implies that nuclear dangers can be eliminated forever, as if the dilemmas of security and the balance of power somehow can be made to disappear.

Related to this myopia is a tendency to perceive disarmament and deterrence as irreconcilable polar opposites. For doves, disarmament is equated with peace, weapons and deterrence with war. Hawks have the opposite view: disarmament is an invitation to war; arms and deterrence are the basis of peace. The competing visions are black and white, and as such they miss the subtleties of perspective that might combine to create a realistic vision of how security can be enhanced without nuclear weapons.

The defenders of continued nuclear deterrence dismiss disarmament as a practical impossibility. You cannot 'uninvent' the bomb, we are told, and to think otherwise is folly. The point is correct of course, but this does not mean that the elimination of nuclear weapons is impossible or impractical. The knowl-edge of how to build nuclear weapons can never be erased, and the materials and technology for doing so will remain part of the human experience, but these realities do not preclude the possibility of taking practical steps to steadily reduce and eliminate nuclear weapons, and to prohibit the development and deployment of such weapons in the future.

The realisation that nuclear capability will never disappear is not an obstacle to achieving disarmament, but a foundation upon which to build a realistic and secure strategy for eliminating these weapons. Disarmament does not remove the reality of deterrence, which will continue in a modified form even in a world without nuclear weapons. In fact, the knowledge and capability for nuclear reconstitution can serve as a kind of weaponless deterrent, along with shared missile defences and cooperative conventional defences, to protect the safety of a world that no longer relies on deployed nuclear weapons. The ability to build nuclear weapons will always exist and can serve as a deterrent and constant reminder to potential aggressors that the attempt to command a nuclear monopoly is bound to fail.

Many argue that even if disarmament were feasible it would be undesirable and dangerous. Nuclear deterrence has helped to keep the peace and its removal might invite renewed war and aggression. Nuclear weapons exist because some states, often located in crisis-ridden regions, inevitably experience threats to their security, and they want to rely on these weapons to defend their sovereignty. The challenges to international security in a system of competing nation-states will not disappear with the removal of a particular type of weapon system.

These are valid points, but they do not diminish the necessity of disarmament. Acknowledgement of fundamental security realities makes nuclear disarmament more, not less, urgent. Reliance on deployed nuclear weapons as a form of deterrence is an imperfect security strategy, not least because it validates the utility of these weapons and spurs proliferation.

Disarmament is ultimately a political process. To reach nuclear zero it is necessary to achieve what Professor Jonathan Schell describes as political zero, a state of political relations among nations in which there is no desire or need to possess nuclear weapons, where tensions and animosities that lead nations to fear their neighbours have declined towards zero.[12] Political zero does not mean that nations live in a world without conflicts; it only means the risks of conflict can be limited in a system where certain mechanisms exist to prerevent them from escalating to dangerous levels.

When political tensions are low, so presumably is the motivation to develop nuclear weapons. The nations of Europe were once hostile and militarily competitive with one another, but they have united in a cooperative political community in which security tensions have diminished towards zero. In Latin America and East Asia, nations have witnessed long periods of relative peace. Cooperative political relations and mutual economic interdependence provide assurances of security, however imperfect, and reduce the likelihood of war and weapons proliferation.

Although political leaders have declared their support for a world without nuclear weapons, widespread doubts remain about the desirability and feasibility of nuclear disarmament. Among the nuclear-weapons states, the strongest advocates of nuclear abolition are the countries that stand to gain the most in relative security and influence (especially the United States and the United Kingdom). Even in these countries, competing mindsets for and against nuclear weapons clash with each other. Changes in domestic power alignments may produce policy reversals that can be quite disruptive and have international repercussions. The United States has traditionally based its military dominance on nuclear weapons, but the new coalition of the Obama administration and the movement sparked by the Shultz initiative appears to perceive the situation differently. The current Russian leadership has committed itself publicly to the vision of a nuclear-free world, but Russia's security doctrine adopted in 2000 underlines the importance of nuclear forces for the nation's defence. Other nuclear-armed states with fewer weapons – China, India and Pakistan – are not at the front line of the nuclear disarmament process, but they also have reservations on the ultimate goal of nuclear abolition.

The prospect of nuclear disarmament is creating new political dividing lines, not only among governments, but increasingly also within them, including in the nuclear-armed states. Members of the nuclear 'club' are not necessarily poised against those that do not possess the bomb in a polarised manner. Indeed, even as the politics of disarmament and non-proliferation becomes more complex, it contains the seeds of new solutions and breakthroughs. To some extent the situation resembles the international debate on climate change, in which the relative positions of countries differ and new coalitions emerge. An important difference is, of course, that on nuclear-weapons issues there are no effective multilateral fora for negotiations, other than the 65-member UN Conference on Disarmament (CD) in Geneva, which a US congressional task force in 2005 described as 'too unwieldy to do serious work'.[13]

Defining disarmament

It is technically feasible to dismantle nuclear weapons and establish necessary verification systems to reach a point of nuclear zero, but this will not eliminate security dilemmas or remove the potential danger of cheating and nuclear breakout. The possibility of governments or non-state actors attempting to acquire and use nuclear weapons will always exist, even in a world where such weapons are no longer deployed and where their production has been banned. Because of these realities deterrence will remain necessary, although in a defensive and non-weaponised form.

Deterrence is built on the capacity to defend against aggression. The defensive posture must be structured, however, so that it does not become a predicate for offence. This has been the historic concern with strategic missile defence and the nuclear offence–defence competition. An effective ballistic-missile defence (BMD) can provide a first-strike capability for a state so long as it has invested enough in offensive missiles. In such circumstances, missile defences can undermine mutually assured destruction, thereby weakening deterrence. To mitigate this threat the US and the USSR agreed to limitations on both offensive weapons and missile defences as far back as 1972, under the Anti-Ballistic Missile (ABM) Treaty.

What does this mean for BMD capabilities? If they remain unrestricted and under unilateral national ownership, the first-strike potential may increase as missile defences become more effective against the smaller number of offensive missiles by other states. Therefore, successful nuclear disarmament requires either the abolition of BMD capabilities or their shared control. The latter approach reflects the vision of Reagan, who argued that cooperative missile-defences would provide reassurance against cheating in a world where nuclear weapons had been eliminated. Cooperative missile-defence arrangements would have to be in place either before the offensive missiles were completely abolished or constructed together after that goal had been reached.

Multiple gradations of MAD are possible. At one end of the spectrum is what can be termed 'cold war' deterrence, the reliance on massive levels of nuclear overkill, sometimes described as maximum deterrence.[14] Cold War deterrence policies were based on the threat of massive nuclear annihilation, a prospect that generated widespread public fear, an almost literal sense of the bomb in the living room. Further along the spectrum is minimum deterrence, which is subject to multiple interpretations but can be generally defined as the smallest number of nuclear weapons sufficient for a credible second-strike capability. This low level is generally estimated today at approximately 100 to 200 weapons for each nuclear weapons state (NWS). This level would be adequate as a deterrent force for retaliatory purposes but insufficient as a potential first-strike force. Today, second-tier nuclear powers have stayed roughly at this level of nuclear armaments.

Minimal deterrence and virtual nuclear deterrence[15] differ, in that weapons are operational in the former, while in the latter they have been disassembled. Once states reach a minimal level of deployed weapons they might agree to a process of separating warheads and launch vehicles in a verified manner so that weapons cannot be used promptly. In this scenario, the weapons would remain available as a possible deterrent if deemed necessary, but a period of time would be needed to mate warheads and delivery vehicles. The possibility of first strike or nuclear accident would be reduced. The role of nuclear weapons in security policy would diminish. The bomb would move to the basement.

Moving further along the spectrum, states might agree to eliminate deployed weapons altogether, but they would retain knowledge and reconstitution capacity, which would serve as a form of weaponless deterrence. The development, testing and use of nuclear weapons would be prohibited, backed up by greatly enhanced international verification and enforcement capacities. The prospect of first strike would recede and the time required for possible nuclear use would lengthen. Nuclear weapons would no longer play an active role in national and international security planning. The bomb would essentially be gone, although its memory would persist and the possibility of its return would cast a permanent shadow over the future, serving as a kind of deterrent to would-be aggressors, even in the absence of actual bombs.

Disarmament is a dynamic process, not an absolute end state. It can be understood as a continuous series of steps to enhance security by reducing reliance on nuclear weapons and minimising the danger of nuclear-weapons development or use. The options include measures to prevent proliferation and reduce nuclear weapons, bans on nuclear testing and fissile-material production, stronger nuclear monitoring and verification requirements, more effective export controls and sanctions on weapons-related goods, and more effective use of multilateral sanctions and incentives. The options also include specific steps to reach nuclear zero and beyond, including agreement on minimal deterrence, procedures for the separation of warheads and launch vehicles (virtual deterrence), agreement on the elimination and dismantlement of remaining nuclear-weapons capabilities (nuclear zero), a prohibition against future nuclear-weapons development or use, the deployment of shared missile defences and agreement on options for monitored reconstitution capacity (weaponless deterrence). Also needed are non-military strategies and policies for resolving armed conflicts and enhancing international security, through more vigorous multilateral peacemaking, greater enforcement of international law, stronger international peacekeeping and policing policies, sustainable economic development and support for democracy and human rights.

This list of required strategies is long and daunting, and it is easy to become discouraged about the prospects of disarmament, but the good news is that many of the listed strategies are already being negotiated or implemented. Policies to prevent nuclear terrorism and proliferation, reductions in nuclear arsenals, a halt to nuclear testing, more rigorous nuclear monitoring systems, more effective export controls and sanctions and incentives-based diplomacy – these and other necessary measures are being implemented today, to varying degrees of effectiveness.

The only untested strategies are those that will become possible after states reduce their nuclear arsenals to zero. That stage of development, which may seem inconceivable at present, will probably become more feasible as weapons levels are reduced, and as the other strategies for security are implemented. As nations reduce their nuclear weapons holdings to levels of minimum deterrence, they may wish to pause and look around, to consider whether the new reality of diminished nuclear dependency is working. They may then decide on the modalities for going all the way down to zero, while deploying shared defences and developing reconstitution protocols that could ensure stability and deterrence at zero levels. All of this would be part of a momentous process of political evolution towards reduced dependency on weapons-based defence and greater reliance on cooperative approaches to security.

The new nuclear moment

The most important requirement for an evolution towards mutual disarmament is political will: a vigorous, sustained commitment by political leaders in the most powerful states to achieve a world without nuclear weapons and implement the steps for getting there. The greatest obstacles to disarmament are not technical but political.

Political will has grown in recent years, propelled by worldwide concern about the twin dangers of nuclear proliferation and the threat of terrorist nuclear attack. Underlying the current surge in support for disarmament, writes Scott Sagan, are complex motives and multiple fears. Chief among these is the belief that disarmament by the nuclear-weapons states is necessary to prevent further proliferation.[16] The urgent need to reduce nuclear dangers has prompted a growing chorus of disarmament statements by world leaders and present and former security officials. Such statements were echoed at the September 2009 special session of the UN Security Council, attended by heads of state and chaired by President Barack Obama, which adopted Resolution 1887 to combat the smuggling, financing and theft of proliferation-related nuclear materials. The resolution called for strengthening the many policies that have been adopted by national governments and international bodies to prevent the spread of nuclear weapons and tighten controls over weapons-related technology and materials.

The current 'neo-abolitionist' movement emerged from an October 2006 conference at the Hoover Institution in California commemorating the twentieth anniversary of the Reykjavik Summit.[17] Soon afterwards Shultz, Kissinger, Perry and Nunn joined together in publishing their now famous article in the *Wall Street Journal* declaring support for the elimination of nuclear weapons and listing necessary steps for achieving that goal. These measures include the reduction of nuclear risk – by increasing warning time, eliminating tactical nuclear weapons and establishing better physical security of nuclear weapons and materials – and the establishment of additional arms control agreements. The latter includes bringing the Comprehensive Test-Ban Treaty (CTBT) into force, making progress on a Fissile Material Cut-Off Treaty (FMCT) and concluding a successor to the Strategic Arms Reduction Treaty.[18]

The Hoover initiative was followed by similar statements by other high-level groups of former officials and leaders in the United Kingdom, Russia, Germany, France, Norway, Poland, Japan, Australia and other countries. Many of the national initiatives, following the model of the original Shultz statement, were non-partisan and cross-party in character, with Democrats joining Republicans in the United States, and conservatives, liberals and social democrats speaking together in Europe and beyond.

These unprecedented high-level commitments to nuclear disarmament have prompted countless conferences and a wide array of civil society initiatives to generate public understanding and support for eliminating nuclear weapons. The new momentum for nuclear abolition is also embodied in the International Commission on Nuclear Non-proliferation and Disarmament, sponsored by the governments of Japan and Australia and chaired by respective former foreign ministers Yoriko Kawaguchi and Gareth Evans, which released its report in December 2009.

For some of the former officials now advocating disarmament, the commitment to nuclear abolition is a striking departure from previous beliefs. Perry had spent most of his professional life in the Pentagon creating and maintaining nuclear weapons. At the end of the Cold War, however, he realised that the vast remaining arsenals of the United States and Russia were a security liability rather than an asset. His support for the elimination of nuclear weapons grew with increasing international concern about the dangerous intersection of proliferation and terrorism. Although the number of nuclear weapons has diminished since the end of the Cold War, the danger of a nuclear device actually exploding in a city somewhere has increased. There are fewer bombs in the world, but they are in a growing number of hands, and they are coveted by those who would not hesitate to use them to inflict maximum casualties and mayhem. Perry told a National Academy of Sciences panel in 2004: 'I have never been as worried as I am now that a nuclear bomb will be detonated in an American city ... I fear that we are racing toward an unprecedented catastrophe'.[19]

Shultz, Perry, Kissinger and Nunn have pointed to the fear of terrorist acquisition of nuclear devices as an important reason to work for nuclear abolition. Many international experts and policy reports have called attention to the threat of nuclear terrorism. The Weapons of Mass Destruction Commission, led by former head of the International Atomic Energy Agency (IAEA) Hans Blix, described the possible terrorist use of nuclear weapons as an increasing threat that could occur 'either within or across state borders'.[20] A 2008 report by the independent commission set up to examine the Agency's role until 2020 noted that 'a sophisticated and well-financed terrorist group that acquired enough highly enriched uranium (HEU) or sepa-rated plutonium might be able to construct a crude nuclear bomb that could incinerate the heart of any of the world's major cities'. The result could be tens of thousands of deaths, widespread economic and social disruption and a serious blow to international security.[21]

Incidents of nuclear smuggling and trafficking have occurred regularly, with small quantities of missing weapons-usable material turning up on the black market. The facilities from which these materials originated did not report them missing, according to former CIA and US Department of Energy offi-cial Rolf Mowatt-Larssen.[22] Controls over sensitive materials at some nuclear sites remain woefully inadequate. Despite the attention devoted to these issues in recent years, no specific binding global standards exist for ensuring the security of nuclear materials.

It is not only fear that has inspired the current concern for reducing and eliminating nuclear weapons. It is also hope, and a desire to rekindle the spirit of transformational denuclearisa-tion that Reagan and Gorbachev embodied in the latter half of the 1980s. For Shultz the commitment to disarmament has been motivated by a desire to return to the Reykjavik agenda, to complete the unfinished business of eliminating nuclear weapons. By calling attention to Reagan's abolitionist vision, Shultz and others have fundamentally transformed the disarmament debate.[23]

Previously the domain of liberals and the political left, the cause of nuclear disarmament has now become identified also with American conservatism. The impact of this broadening of the political base was reflected in the 2008 presidential campaign in the United States during which both candidates vowed support for nuclear abolition. Republican candidate John McCain stated: 'A quarter of a century ago, President Ronald Reagan declared, "Our dream is to see the day when nuclear weapons will be banished from the face of the Earth." That is my dream, too.'[24] His invocation of Reagan's abolitionist vision has generated hope for a disarmament movement that transcends political and ideological differences. Politics can, indeed, create strange bedfellows.

Support for a world without nuclear weapons also reflects a consciousness of the global threats to the viability of human life. In commenting on the deeper meanings of the nuclear age, Hans Morgenthau once wrote that 'death is the great scandal' in human experience, but that nuclear death 'destroys the meaning of life' itself by jeopardising the very existence of society and history. Following Morgenthau's logic, one could say that nuclear war would be the 'great scandal' in the experience of human history.[25]

Several observers have noted parallels in the concern about nuclear dangers and the deepening public awareness of the threats posed by climate change and global environmental degradation. Jonathan Schell has spoken of a 'coming of age' of humankind, an increasing awareness of our human capacity to destroy ourselves and ruin the natural environment upon which all life depends.[26] Whether this danger of self-destruction is realised quickly through nuclear Armageddon or gradually through environmental ruin, the ultimate fate and threat to life is the same. To address these collective, self-imposed dangers requires not only a new awareness but a new sense of collective social responsibility. Efforts to reduce and eliminate nuclear weapons can be considered part of that broader social responsibility, elements of a moral and political commitment to protect life and preserve the planet.

At the dawn of the atomic age those responsible for inventing the bomb understood its momentous political consequences and attempted to abolish such weapons. Initiatives to control the power of the atom foundered, however, on the suspicions of great-power competition. Later calls for general and complete disarmament became a political ritual rather than a serious effort to stop the arms race. Only the frightening escalation of nuclear competition and accompanying political risks alerted the United States and the Soviet Union to the need for controlling and managing nuclear arms.

In the 1980s, the first steps of a new departure were taken by Presidents Gorbachev and Reagan, who seriously considered completely dismantling nuclear weapons. They did not succeed, but the precedent of Reykjavik has inspired new momentum for abolition. The present movement towards a nuclear-free world arises in a very different international context. The bipolar world of 1986 has been replaced by a more multipolar system in which economic resources are distributed and new centres of power, including new nuclear-weapons states, have emerged. This entails the risk that nuclear devices may fall into the hands of terrorists.

The road to nuclear zero will be long, almost certainly taking decades rather than years. Reaching the destination will require substantial reforms and changes. Nuclear deterrence will continue but in a less weaponised form, as a back-up to which states can return if their security is in jeopardy. Deterrence will be virtual, in the sense that the means for immediate use of nuclear weapons will not exist, but retaliatory capacity will remain based on reconstitution ability. Expanded monitoring and verification systems will be in place to provide greater capacity to detect cheating or breakout. Shared defences will be deployed to provide means of countering rogue nuclear-missile threats. In these and other ways the abolition of nuclear weapons will be built on the firm foundations of political realism.

CHAPTER TWO

Challenges to the Non-proliferation Regime

The global non-proliferation regime has withstood major challenges over the decades and remains an essential pillar of international security. The Nuclear Non-proliferation Treaty (NPT) has faced many criticisms, but the fact remains that the treaty has prevented the cascade of proliferation feared in the 1960s and 1970s, when it was commonplace to predict that some two dozen countries would possess nuclear explosives by 2000. Only four countries have joined the group of nuclear-weapons states since the treaty was concluded.

The assessment of the NPT can be framed in hypothetical terms: what might have happened if it had not been in existence? The treaty played a role in stopping proliferation activities that were under way in the late 1960s and crystallised decisions in key states – especially Germany, Japan, Sweden and Switzerland – not to manufacture nuclear weapons. On the other hand, several committed outsiders – India, Israel and Pakistan – never contemplated joining the treaty and proceeded to develop the bomb. Others hedged their nuclear bets by joining the Treaty while continuing in secret to develop a nuclear weapons capability. The direct impact of the treaty is therefore mixed, according to former US ambassador to the NPT Review Conference Lewis Dunn. Many would-be nuclear-armed states, he says, decided to give up the nuclear-weapons option, but others continued to exercise it under the nose of the International Atomic Energy Agency (IAEA). The Treaty nonetheless reinforced the emerging non-nuclear norm and gave the international community a stronger legal mandate to inspect potential violations and apply corrective and punitive measures.[1]

The structure of the NPT has evolved considerably since it came into force 40 years ago, although certain inequalities within the treaty regime continue to create dilemmas for maintaining political support and compliance. An inherent tension exists between the treaty's guarantee of the right to develop nuclear energy and the challenge of maintaining a separation between peaceful and military uses of the atom. This task may become more difficult in coming years as nuclear energy production increases. Gaining control over the nuclear fuel cycle has been a priority since the beginning of the atomic age, yet solutions that respect state sovereignty and the right to nuclear energy remain elusive. The nuclear-weapons states are required by the treaty to negotiate for disarmament, but many question whether this obligation is being fulfilled. Resolving these and other challenges will be necessary to sustain the global non-proliferation regime and achieve progress towards disarmament.

NPT purpose and history

The NPT regime is built on a triad of measures defining non-proliferation (Articles I–III), the peaceful use of nuclear energy (Articles IV and V) and nuclear disarmament (Article VI). All are part of a grand bargain to accommodate different international interests. All are necessary building blocks of the regime, and the removal of any one of them would lead to its collapse.

Article IV refers to the 'inalienable right of all the Parties to the Treaty to develop research, production and use of nuclear energy for peaceful purposes without discrimination'. During the 1960s, when the NPT was negotiated, scientists were filled with technological optimism on the benefits of nuclear power as a cheap, presumably inexhaustible source of energy and a driver of industrialisation and economic growth. No country of consequence wanted to be left behind in the acquisition and development of nuclear power.

One projection at the time predicted that 'nuclear power will become a mighty industry', partly because of increasing oil prices and the availability of new technologies such as the breeder reactor.[2] Those projections were not realistic, and did not consider the high costs of nuclear-energy production or the political backlash that developed against it. The nuclear enthusiasm of the time explains why access to peaceful nuclear energy had to become one of the cornerstones of the NPT. Now, with nuclear energy demand rising in some parts of the world, especially in Asia, Article IV may gain renewed significance.

The NPT resulted from a joint draft treaty submitted by the United States and the Soviet Union to the Eighteen Nations Committee on Disarmament (known as the ENDC) in Geneva. The US commitment to negotiating the treaty reflected the recommendations of the Gilpatric Committee in 1965, which urged President Lyndon B. Johnson to put non-proliferation high on the political agenda. This was in contrast to the effort just a few years earlier to establish a Multilateral Force (MLF) that would have given to US allies in Europe and Asia partial control of the nuclear weapons being deployed on their territory. The renunciation of the MLF plan was a condition for Soviet approval of the NPT because it deprived West Germany of a nuclear-weapons option.

The first drafts of the treaty did not contain disarmament or peaceful nuclear-energy provisions, which meant that Moscow and Washington wanted simply to ban the spread of nuclear weapons without any concessions. Their motivation was to enhance their relative international position by trying to prevent the rise of powers with comparable capability, which might have altered their pre-eminence as bipolar managers of the global balance of power. The admission of the UK, France and China into the club of nuclear-armed states recognised the fact that by the date of the treaty they had already acquired and tested nuclear weapons. Their nuclear forces were deemed acceptable because they did not challenge the global dominance of the two powers.

An unequal burden

Some non-aligned countries have criticised the discriminatory character of the NPT. Critics on the left assert that the treaty is a 'blatantly hypocritical and inequitable instrument'.[3] The notion that the burdens apply equally to all parties is, of course, a myth, since states start with very different capabilities and their obligations under the Treaty vary. The unequal provisions of the treaty jeopardise its effectiveness and have generated widespread resentment and discontent.

The key distinction in the treaty is between nuclear-weapons states (NWS) and non-nuclear weapons states (NNWS). The latter agree to renounce the acquisition of nuclear weapons, while the five initial NWS are recognised as possessing these weapons, although they are required to negotiate for disarmament under Article VI. The treaty does not contain any sanctions against the NWS if they fail in their disarmament obligations.

Prohibitions and obligations of the NPT fall more heavily on NNWS. For the NWS many nuclear activities are permitted based on national decisions rather than international supervision. IAEA safeguards and intrusive inspection requirements apply only to NNWS, for whom any resulting issues of sovereignty and commercial position must be subordinate.

A more subtle but also important discrimination exists in the treaty's Article IV provision for universal access to peaceful nuclear energy, and the obligation of states to cooperate towards that end. As Harald Müller observes, the operation of this article is based on an inherent inequality between technological haves and have-nots.[4] Only the more highly industrialised countries and nuclear-weapons states are capable of the cooperation envisioned in the treaty. Technologically advanced states are the only sources of nuclear technology and reactor fuel that can be made available legally to governments seeking to develop nuclear energy. Thus, the path of autonomous development of nuclear industry is long and costly, and as Iran has experienced, may engender international hostility and sanctions. Most countries choose not to take this route and rely instead on the support and cooperation of the more industrially capable supplier states and a handful of multinational companies that manufacture and operate reactors. This makes the nuclear industry one of the most unequal in the world.

Because developing countries depend on the industrialised world and the nuclear-weapons states to achieve civilian nuclear energy, they may be less inclined to challenge the major powers on questionable nuclear-related policies, such as the US–India nuclear deal. On the other hand, they may further resent the inequality within the NPT regime, and demand more universal, non-discriminatory non-proliferation mechanisms. These concerns about uneven obligations and capabilities create scepticism in the global South towards proposals for multinationalising the nuclear fuel cycle. They also affect the willingness of states to comply with heightened IAEA monitoring and control proposals such as the 1997 Additional Protocol, which gives the agency's inspectors greater access to nuclear sites in countries that have signed it.

Keeping Nuclear Energy Peaceful

It is often argued that nuclear-weapons capability is the conjoined twin of peaceful nuclear energy. The technologies, materials and scientific skills required for developing civilian nuclear energy make it possible for states so inclined to embark on the path of nuclear-weapons development. IAEA safeguards are designed to prevent 'the diversion of nuclear energy from peaceful uses to nuclear weapons'. Its control regime does not prohibit uranium enrichment or plutonium reprocessing as long as they are under IAEA safeguards. This makes the borderline between civilian and military uses the key focus of the inspection regime. It also creates technical difficulty and political uncertainty as to the nature of a contested nuclear programme such as that of Iran.

All the states that have acquired nuclear-weapons capability outside the constraints of the NPT have done so by relying on external assistance and diverting technologies, materials and technical skills from their civilian nuclear programmes. Given the dualistic nature of nuclear technology, the combination of spreading nuclear industry and growing international access to nuclear materials increases proliferation risks. As nuclear technologies mature and spread more widely, so does the capability of building nuclear weapons.

Global reliance on nuclear energy is growing, the result of rising energy demand and concerns about climate change. Sustaining economic growth rates around the world will require a tripling of electricity production, according to the report of the independent commission to the IAEA. Today, 439 nuclear power plants operate in 30 countries and provide approximately 15% of the world's electricity.[5] That number is likely to grow in the years ahead. More than 50 reactors are under construction and many more are in the planning stage. Of those under construction, most are located in just four countries – China, India, Russia and South Korea.[6]

Article IV of the NPT describes unimpeded access to peaceful uses of nuclear energy as an 'inalienable' right of all nations. The right to nuclear energy is conditional, however, and is dependent on a state's commitment to non-proliferation and, it can be argued, full compliance with IAEA safeguards.[7] It is interesting to note that this claim to an 'inalienable' right (without mention of non-proliferation obligations) is exactly the language chanted in pro-government rallies organised by the Iranian regime to protest against foreign attempts to constrain its nuclear programme. The crucial requirement for would-be proliferators is obtaining fissile material. The knowledge of how to make a bomb is readily available, as is the capacity to manufacture bomb components. The greatest technical challenge is acquiring or manufacturing nuclear weapons fuel. These obstacles have eased, however, as centrifuge enrichment and reprocessing technologies have become increasingly available around the world.

As reliance on nuclear energy rises, so does the demand for nuclear fuel, along with the need for enrichment and fuel-fabrication capabilities. The challenge of gaining greater control over the nuclear fuel cycle has emerged as a major non-proliferation concern. There is growing international interest in multilateral solutions to prevent the diversion of nuclear fuel from civilian to military uses through the establishment of viable regional fuel banks and international fuel cycles.[8] Various proposals have been offered for nuclear fuel guarantees and multinational nuclear enrichment arrangements, but these have been met by scepticism. The unwillingness of rising powers such as South Africa, Argentina and Brazil to endorse such proposals reflects their lingering distrust of the major powers and a determination to exercise full sovereignty in developing the capability to produce nuclear energy.

Article VI and the NPT

The basic idea of the 'grand bargain' at the heart of the NPT is the obligation of the NWS to 'pursue negotiations in good faith' as a concession for other states to give up the nuclear-weapons option. In the absence of a timeline for negotiations, however, a 'time inconsistency problem' arises. Non-nuclear states agree now to eschew these weapons, while the five recognised NWS negotiate for disarmament in the future. This inconsistency is addressed in the NPT by Article X, which states that '25 years after the entry into force of the Treaty [in 1995], a conference shall be convened to decide whether the Treaty shall continue in force indefinitely, or shall be extended for an additional fixed period or periods'. That review conference was to be a testing point on whether the basic bargain was still valid. At the 1995 conference, the United States and other nuclear states promised the 'determined pursuit ... of systematic and progressive efforts to reduce nuclear weapons globally, with the ultimate goal of eliminating those weapons'.[9] The inclusion of that language in the conference final statement was a condition for the indefinite extension of the treaty.

The demand for nuclear disarmament and its practical implementation has been stressed by the non-nuclear weapons states since the first NPT Review Conference in Geneva in 1975 and in every conference since then. There has been a widespread argument spearheaded by Mexico, Sweden, Ireland and other members of the so-called Middle Powers Initiative, that the five nuclear-weapons states have not sufficiently honoured their part of the bargain.[10]

Officials in the United States and other nuclear-weapons states respond to these criticisms by pointing to the large reductions in nuclear stockpiles that have been achieved since the end of the Cold War. The number of strategic nuclear weapons deployed by the United States and Russia has declined by approximately 80% over the past two decades. The United Kingdom and France have reduced their arsenals by equivalent percentages, while China has maintained a minimum deterrent posture. However, many NNWS are dissatisfied. They contrast the almost universal agreement (by 184 states) to refrain from nuclear acquisition with the continued possession of these weapons by the NWS. They want an end to nuclear discrimination and more rapid progress towards disarmament.

At the 2000 NPT Review Conference, the nuclear weapons states committed themselves to an 'unequivocal undertaking' to 'accomplish the total elimination of their nuclear arsenals'. They also agreed to take 13 'practical steps' to fulfill the NPT's disarmament obligation. Few of these steps have been implemented. The 2005 NPT Review Conference collapsed in disagreement when the United States refused even to discuss these steps. This disregard for disarmament pledges causes 'festering resentment' over 'double standards', according to the report of the independent commission set up to examine the IAEA's role.[11] Many states are critical of what they see as deliberate efforts to 'perpetuate the inequities of the nonproliferation regime'. This resentment makes it difficult to agree on steps that are urgently needed to strengthen global efforts to stop the spread of nuclear weapons. Any suggestion that NPT reviews should focus solely on non-proliferation and that 'talking about disarmament distracts attention from nonproliferation ... is demonstrably false'.[12]

The key question for the future is whether the goals of nonproliferation can be realigned more effectively with those of nuclear disarmament, especially now that a new political atmosphere conducive to disarmament has emerged. Russia and the United States have made deep cuts in their nuclear arsenals, with further cuts on the way. Saving the NPT was not the main motivation for these reductions, but they nonetheless facilitate that task and create a positive atmosphere for progress on non-proliferation. Historical analysis suggests that the failure of disarmament has not been a main driver of proliferation. Nonetheless states acquiring nuclear weapons have criticised the major powers for their continued reliance on these weapons and have used this argument as a justification for their pursuit of the bomb.

Proliferation

The NWS continue to deploy thousands of weapons, many of them still on active status. They are modernising and upgrading their weapons systems and developing new missions for their potential use. In the 1990s the United States developed a counter-proliferation doctrine envisioning the possible use of nuclear weapons against governments and non-state actors seeking to acquire weapons of mass destruction (WMD).[13] According to this doctrine, nuclear weapons serve not merely to deter and retaliate against possible nuclear attack, but to strike first if necessary against threats posed by the development of WMD. Similar doctrinal shifts have occurred in Russia, the United Kingdom and France. In 1993 Russia abandoned the Soviet-era policy of no first use and declared that nuclear weapons could be used in the event of an overwhelming conventional attack against its armed forces. In 2006 French President Jacques Chirac included the safeguarding of strategic supplies as a vital national interest for which nuclear deterrence could serve a role.[14]

The new missions are major factors in sustaining domestic political and institutional support for nuclear weapons.

They contradict the principle of security guarantees, which are pledges not to use nuclear weapons against non-nuclear states. They are obstacles to achieving an unequivocal commitment from political and security officials for the elimination of nuclear weapons.

Nuclear weapons are considered tools of counter-proliferation, but evidence suggests that nuclear weapons themselves cause proliferation. Their very existence is an inducement to acquisition: the possession of nuclear weapons by one state impels another to seek the same capability. Jonathan Schell has identified what he terms the 'proliferance' effect of nuclear weapons. When a country acquires or seeks nuclear weapons it prompts other states to seek countervailing capability. 'Whereas deterrence stops states in possession of nuclear arsenals from using them, proliferance inspires nations that lack them to get them.'[15] US Secretary of State Hillary Clinton made a similar point in remarks at the US Institute of Peace in Washington in October 2009: 'The nuclear status quo is neither desirable nor sustainable. It gives other countries the motivation or the excuse to pursue their own nuclear options.'[16]

The possession of nuclear weapons by the major powers confers legitimacy on these weapons as the ultimate instruments of national power and prestige. They are the coin of the realm in international politics. Their status as symbols of global influence is reinforced by the fact that the five permanent members of the UN Security Council are the world's only recognised nuclear-weapons states. It is not an accident that India demands simultaneously a permanent seat in the Council and recognition as a nuclear-weapons power as a condition for entering the NPT.

This continued linkage between nuclear-weapons possession and global power encourages proliferation, according to the report of the independent commission to the IAEA. 'If nuclear weapons continue to be seen as offering security and prestige, and states that maintain them continue to send the message that nuclear weapons are essential to security, more states may seek such weapons.' When the world's most powerful states indicate that they consider nuclear weapons essential for their security, the report argues, 'they strengthen the hand of nuclear advocates everywhere'.[17]

In almost every case where states have developed nuclear weapons, they have done so in response to nuclear-weapons development by a rival or neighbouring state and to assert international influence. This pattern has been at work throughout the atomic age. The United States launched the *Manhattan Project* to guard against the possibility that Nazi Germany might develop the bomb. The Soviet Union quickly learned of the US programme and infiltrated spies to purloin nuclear know-how. After the bombing of Hiroshima, Stalin ordered his bomb builders to accelerate the incipient Soviet programme.[18] The nuclear programmes of the United States and the Soviet Union prompted China's decision to develop the bomb. The United Kingdom and France developed their nuclear programmes not only as a deterrent against the Soviet threat but as a means of maintaining their great-power status. British Prime Minister Harold Macmillan said in 1957 that independent nuclear capability would solidify the UK's special relationship with the United States and 'our influence in world affairs'. His French counterpart Michel Debré similarly considered nuclear weapons necessary to assert France's 'influence in international life'.[19] India decided to 'exercise the nuclear option' to counter Chinese power and gain global influence, which prompted Pakistan to follow suit. North Korea and Iran have developed their nuclear capabilities in part to deter US military threats.

The perils of pre-emption

The challenges of sustaining necessary cooperation for arms reduction are made more difficult by the legacy of the unilateralist policies of the George W. Bush administration. These policies were based on a selective non-proliferation strategy that focuses on the actions of particular actors rather than the general problem of nuclear development. This strategy exposed differences between those who see the bomb itself as the problem and those who perceive specific countries as the main threat. Michael Krepon argued that the general view, in which norms are meant to apply universally, was the original intention of the NPT.[20] The Bush administration adopted a different approach, limiting its attention to countries 'behaving badly', and even rewarding proliferation behaviour in states it deemed reliable strategic allies (as seen in its nuclear deal with India).

The policies of preventive war on display in the 2003 invasion of Iraq opened many wounds in international politics that have left lasting scars. The war contributed to regional and global insecurities, exacerbating the very conditions that often impel countries to seek greater military and nuclear capabilities. The Obama administration has made concerted efforts to mend fences and convey a new era of internationalism in US policy, but the damage created by the previous administration will not be easily repaired. The US reputation for world leadership has been badly damaged, especially in the Muslim world, and the institutions and norms of multilateralism have been weakened. The chaos and aftermath of the Iraq War will have continuing unintended consequences, exacerbating proliferation dynamics in the region and beyond. The declaration of an 'axis of evil', followed by the invasion of Iraq, sent a clear message to Iran and other would-be proliferators: don't wait to get the bomb if you want to avoid Saddam Hussein's fate.[21] By installing a

Shi'ite-led, Iran-friendly government in Baghdad, the coalition enhanced Tehran's geopolitical position in the region. The neglect of arms-control dialogue with North Korea for several years entrenched the isolation of the Pyongyang regime and enabled it to accumulate additional nuclear weapons material. The alienation of Russia and China on security issues damaged the prospects for great-power cooperation, which in many respects is the most important requirement for achieving global progress on denuclearisation. These and other legacies of the Bush administration will be difficult to overcome and have made the path towards multilateral disarmament more arduous.

Disputes over the acquisition of nuclear weapons have created some of the most dangerous moments in history, notably the Cuban Missile Crisis, and they continue to pose a grave danger to international security. Disputes over proliferation of nuclear weapons are potentially major sources of global insecurity. They were used to rationalise war and military strikes in Iraq. The continuing confrontation with Iran over its nuclear programmes is a source of acute insecurity in the region and globally. It shows that nuclear weapons can cause war even when they are not used, and in the case of Iraq, even when they do not exist.

Conclusion

The challenges to denuclearisation are formidable but not necessarily insoluble. Some problems are inherent to the NPT system. The tension between civilian and military uses of atomic energy is unavoidable, and requires continuous verification efforts to detect and prevent diversion from one use to the other. Most of the problems are political in nature. Solutions depend on the quality of relations between nations and the nature of policies within states. Both the major powers and non-aligned states have roles to play: the latter through an acceptance of multinational fuel guarantees and robust verification systems, the former through the alignment of nuclear policy with disarmament pledges and support for a more equitable non-proliferation regime. Progress towards disarmament, writes political scientist Scott Sagan, will require 'a coordinated global effort of shared responsibilities among NWS and NNWS'.[22] It is difficult to imagine how the NWS can be serious about non-proliferation while they cling to strategies of possible nuclear use and military pre-emption. The core bargain at the heart of the NPT is inescapable: preventing proliferation means achieving disarmament. One is not possible without the other.

CHAPTER THREE

Why States Give up the Bomb

Non-proliferation efforts have succeeded more often than they have failed. Over the years many more states have given up nuclear-weapons programmes than now possess or are developing them.[1] According to Joseph Cirincione, president of the Ploughshares Fund (a charitable foundation that focuses on nuclear-weapons policy), in the 1960s 23 states had nuclear programmes, were conducting weapons-related research or were actively discussing the pursuit of nuclear weapons. Today only ten states have or are believed to be seeking nuclear weapons and five of these are the declared nuclear-weapons states (NWS) of the NPT. Before the Treaty came into force, only six nations had abandoned nuclear-weapons programmes that were under way or being considered. Since then 16 countries have abandoned programmes. No nation has initiated a nuclear weapons programme since the end of the Cold War, the North Korean and Iranian programmes having begun in the 1980s.[2] The record shows a significant success rate for the NPT in stemming the spread of nuclear weapons.

The following table, drawn from Paul Davis's analysis for the International Commission on Non-proliferation and Nuclear Disarmament, depicts these developments:

States possessing or seeking nuclear weapons:	
Currently known to have nuclear weapons:	
Recognised by the NPT:	Not recognised by the NPT:
China	India
France	Israel
Russia	North Korea
United Kingdom	Pakistan
United States	
Suspected programme:	
	Iran
Suspected aspiration:	
	Syria
States formerly possessing or seeking nuclear weapons:	
Own weapons given up:	
	South Africa
Inherited weapons given up:	
	Belarus
	Kazakhstan
	Ukraine
Consideration or weapons research voluntarily terminated:	
Argentina	Romania
Australia	South Korea
Brazil	Spain
Canada	Sweden
Egypt	Switzerland
Italy	Taiwan
Indonesia	West Germany
Japan	Yugoslavia
Norway	
Programme terminated through negotiation:	
	Libya
Programme terminated under coercive pressure:	
	Iraq

Understanding the reasons for nuclear reversal is crucial to comprehending the conditions that will be necessary for creating a world without nuclear weapons. This is relevant because the countries relinquishing the bomb have created new political space in an international context that previously did not favour nuclear abdication. If the process of nuclear disarmament moves ahead, decisions to forgo nuclear weapons in the future can take place in a more receptive environment.[3]

Determinants of denuclearisation

Studies by T.V. Paul, Etel Solingen, Ariel Levite, Mitchell Reiss, Harald Müller and others have examined the nuclear rollback phenomenon in detail. They have analysed why certain states have halted development programmes or dismantled weapons they either developed or inherited. These studies reveal a wide variety of motivations for decisions to give up the bomb, but they all identify a recurring set of primary factors that are common to cases of nuclear reversal.[4] The first and most important is an improvement in the security situation so that nuclear weapons are no longer deemed necessary. The second is a shift in domestic political governance towards greater democracy, market liberalisation and global integration. The third is the presence of external incentives, often provided by the United States, that diminish the appeal of nuclear weapons.[5] All of these factors work together to dissuade a government from going nuclear.

A recent quantitative analysis by Müller and Andreas Schmidt identifies the correlates of nuclear reversal.[6] The authors reviewed all cases since 1945 in which states developed or considered nuclear-weapons programmes (37 in all). They examined the decisions to terminate or continue nuclear programmes according to a range of variables, including the political characteristics of a regime, technological imperatives, alliance guarantees and the role of non-proliferation norms. Their analysis concurred with other studies in identifying security issues as primary factors in determining nuclear decision-making. They also identified regime type and non-proliferation norms as important influences. Their findings challenged the common assumption that alliance guarantees are important factors in shaping nuclear decision-making. Moreover, they found no evidence of an association between economic and technological capability and the decision to develop nuclear weapons.[7]

The lack of a strong correlation between non-proliferation and alliance guarantees is the most striking finding of Müller and Schmidt's analysis. This runs counter to the common assumption that security guarantees from nuclear-weapons states are essential in convincing states to refrain from weapons development. Many believe that the US policy of extended deterrence, the so-called nuclear umbrella, has been decisive in dissuading states in East Asia and Europe from going nuclear. To test this hypothesis Müller and Schmidt compared the behaviour of US allies in Europe, East and Southeast Asia and the Pacific with that of non-aligned countries in the same regions. In a sample of 31 states they found no statistically significant difference in the proliferation behaviour of allies and non-aligned states. Neither did they find any confirmation of the presumed linkage between alliance guarantees and decisions not to develop nuclear weapons.

This finding can be interpreted in several different ways. Either the allies did not consider security assurances based on nuclear deterrence credible, or non-aligned countries felt that the US nuclear umbrella protected them as well. Perhaps extended nuclear deterrence is essentially irrelevant to non-proliferation. In any case, the finding casts doubt on one of the pillars of deterrence theory and a principal justification for maintaining nuclear deployments to protect allies.

Solingen argues that the limits of deterrence assurance apply to hegemonic defence relationships generally. Neither the United States nor the Soviet Union was able to prevent allies (Israel, Iran under the Shah, Iraq or North Korea) from seeking or acquiring nuclear-weapons capability. Most nuclear reversals are not due to the US nuclear umbrella.[8] If alliance guarantees are so effective in restraining allies, sceptics ask, why did the United Kingdom and France develop nuclear weapons?

This analysis does not mean that alliance guarantees play no role whatsoever. It is undeniable, as Müller and Schmidt acknowledge, that Japan, Germany and other states have made decisions not to develop nuclear weapons based in part on alliances with and security guarantees from the United States. The causal relationship may not be as straightforward as commonly assumed, however. Perhaps it is not nuclear deterrence per se but the importance of the political alliance relationship that matters most in dissuading states from going nuclear, although of course the two are interrelated.

Müller and Schmidt also examined the relationship between denuclearisation and non-proliferation. They tested the hypothesis that great-power arsenals deter smaller states from proliferating – which implies that as the major states disarm, the marginal value of small arsenals will increase and incentives for proliferation will rise. Their analysis found little support for this hypothesis. During periods of arms control and détente, proliferation activities diminished, and the number of decisions to terminate nuclear weapons increased. In the most dangerous periods of the Cold War, the number of countries initiating nuclear-weapons programmes increased. During the 'second Cold War' of the early 1980s, when US and Soviet nuclear arsenals expanded, the rate of proliferation increased slightly. With the end of the Cold War and the deep nuclear reductions of the late 1980s and early 1990s, nuclear proliferation activities declined sharply. No new nuclear programme started after that date, but several were terminated.

Nuclear non-proliferation is also linked to reduced threats from chemical and biological weapons. The decline in the number of nuclear-weapons programmes globally has been accompanied by a drop in the number of programmes for the development of chemical and biological weapons and ballistic missiles. As Cirincione observes, 'the number of nuclear, biological, and chemical weapons and ballistic missiles [is] shrinking steadily. The number of states with programmes for these weapons is also contracting'.[9] It is difficult to establish any causal relationship between these trends except to note the contextual influence. Changes in the international institutional and normative environment encourage reductions in military capabilities and discourage the acquisition of new weapons systems.[10]

Müller and Schmidt found support for the hypothesis that domestic regime characteristics are important in determining proliferation behaviour. The presence of democratic and democratising regimes is positively correlated with decisions not to develop or possess nuclear weapons. This confirms Solingen's pioneering research on the importance of domestic factors in accounting for proliferation and non-proliferation behaviour. Her research shows that the political and ideological characteristics of a ruling regime are significant predictive factors in determining whether a state will embrace or eschew nuclear-weapons capability. Nationalist, autocratic and autarkic regimes are more likely to develop nuclear weapons, while democratic regimes oriented towards market liberalisation tend to be less likely to develop such weapons. The change from one regime type to the other is associated in several important cases with the decision to abandon nuclear-weapons capability.

This does not mean that democracies are inherently non-nuclear, of course. Established democracies that have invested heavily in and maintained nuclear weapons for prolonged periods – the United States, the United Kingdom, France, Israel and now India – obviously have not abandoned their programmes. As George Perkovich demonstrated in his analysis of the Indian nuclear programme, democracies can be susceptible to nationalist and patriotic political appeals to go nuclear.[11] The democratic peace phenomenon does not extend to questions of nuclear-weapons acquisition.

The non-proliferation norm

The international non-proliferation norms embodied in the NPT have had a positive impact in constraining nuclear-weapons development and persuading states to abandon nuclear programmes. Prior to the NPT entering into force in 1970, 40% of the states possessing the requisite economic and technical capacity embarked on programmes to develop nuclear weapons capability. After 1970, as international political opinion decisively embraced non-proliferation standards, most of the states that started nuclear weapons programmes terminated them, and few of the states with requisite capacity started nuclear weapons programmes. Some countries abandoned weapons programmes to fulfill obligations under the NPT, while others were less explicit in their declared motivations. In the former case the positive impact of the treaty was obvious, while in others it had to be inferred from the context.

Müller and Schmidt explain this phenomenon by arguing that democracies are more sensitive to norm formation. The emerging global norm of nuclear renunciation is more influential in states that are oriented towards democracy and open markets.[12] As the number of democratic states has increased, so has the receptivity to widely supported non-proliferation norms.

Mitchell Reiss argues the international non-proliferation regime played a role in the decisions of South Africa, Ukraine,

Belarus and Kazakhstan to forgo nuclear weapons. It also helped to motivate the decisions of Argentina and Brazil to abandon nuclear-weapons development. For these countries, 'joining the NPT was the non-proliferation equivalent of obtaining the Good Housekeeping seal of approval'. It was the gold standard for gaining diplomatic acceptance and achieving improved diplomatic and commercial relations with the international community.[13] As noted below, acceptance of the NPT was the essential condition for these regimes to receive economic, diplomatic and security support.

In the cases of Ukraine, Belarus and Kazakhstan the decision to 'send home' Soviet missiles and warheads was connected with their quest for genuine sovereignty. Nuclear weapons were considered a Soviet legacy that was more of a nuisance than an asset in the international community they wanted to enter. Nuclear weapons were in the hands of the Soviet military and technical experts, reminding the local people of their imperial function. Moreover, the Russian Federation and the United States agreed that it was safer to move the weapons to Moscow's custody rather than risk them falling into other hands.

Tools of persuasion

The history of non-proliferation teaches that nations must be persuaded to give up nuclear weapons. Sustainable disarmament cannot be enforced through sheer coercion or physical denial. Political leaders must acquire an internalised belief that nuclear weapons are illegitimate and counterproductive. Positive inducements are likely to be more effective in this process than negative sanctions. Coercive disarmament worked only once, in the exceptional case of Iraq, which was defeated in war and subject to draconian multilateral sanctions. In other cases approaches that relied excessively on pressure and threats of force usually failed. Nations give up nuclear weapons only when they feel they have more to gain in the process than they might lose. These are calculations that states must make for themselves; they cannot be imposed externally.[14] The domestic calculus of the expected costs and benefits is decisive for the outcome of decision-making. Actors tend to change their behaviour on the basis of expected utilities and external inducements rather than penalties.

This does not mean that sanctions have no role to play in achieving non-proliferation and disarmament. Sanctions have helped in some cases in raising the price and slowing the progress of nuclear-weapons development. Sanctions contribute to the effectiveness of incentives by working in combination with them. The offer to lift sanctions can serve as a potent inducement for cooperation. Sanctions and incentives are often applied in combination as part of a diplomatic bargaining process designed to reach mutual agreement. The art of diplomacy lies in creatively blending pressures and inducements to exert persuasive influence and reward a state for adopting a desired change in policy.[15]

Studies confirm the advantages of inducement policies and the benefits of combining incentives with sanctions as tools of diplomatic persuasion. Virginia Foran and Leonard Spector found that incentives are not usually offered by themselves, but are part of a package of incentives and disincentives designed to affect a state's decision-making calculus. An incentives–disincentives package is 'a set of promised benefits and threatened sanctions' that seeks to discourage a state from developing or maintaining nuclear weapons.[16]

Analysts have observed a strong positive correlation between policy success and the utilisation of incentives in combination with sanctions. Empirical evidence shows that inducement policies are more successful than sanctions, and

that the combination of incentives and sanctions is more effective than the use of incentives alone.[17] In practice incentives
and disincentives are difficult to distinguish in a particular
case. The offer to lift sanctions is an incentive, while the denial
of economic or diplomatic inducements is a sanction.

In some cases non-proliferation incentives packages have
resembled a modernised version of dollar diplomacy, with
financial and commercial incentives used to restrain nuclear
behaviour.[18] The United States has been the primary practi-
tioner of this form of diplomacy, but Japan, Germany, Russia
and other countries have also used economic assistance to
promote non-proliferation and security objectives. Incentives
have been combined in some instances with denial strategies, which seek to prevent weapons-trafficking. Strict export
controls on nuclear technologies and materials are now
in place in many countries, especially the members of the
Nuclear Suppliers Group (NSG). The use of sanctions can be
helpful in stemming the flow of weapons-related materials
and imposing costs on proliferators, but by themselves denial
strategies are inadequate. Leon Sigal, a northeast Asia security expert, observes:

> Denial can buy time and provide early warning, but
> it cannot succeed forever. The interdiction of supply
> has to be supplemented by efforts to reduce demand.
> Unlike a strategy of pure denial, which threatens
> proliferators with economic and political isolation,
> convincing countries not to build a bomb requires
> cooperating with them, however unsavory that may
> be. Countries that seek nuclear arms are insecure.
> Trying to isolate them or force them to forgo nuclear
> arming could well backfire. They need reassurance to
> ease their insecurity.[19]

The best approach, according to Sigal, is a 'strategy of diplomatic give-and-take that combines reassurance with conditional reciprocity, promising inducements on the condition that potential proliferators accept nuclear restraints'.

Lessons from Brazil and Argentina

The influence of domestic political factors in nuclear renunciation is clearly illustrated in the cases of Argentina and Brazil. Of decisive importance was the emergence in the 1980s of civilian governments in Argentina (1983) and Brazil (1985) determined to wrest control over nuclear programmes from their military establishments. The return to civilian rule ushered in a new political era that facilitated the establishment of more cooperative political relations, leading both countries to perceive the nuclear-weapons option as an impediment to regional stability and security. The development of mutual trust and transparency had started already during the military regimes, but accelerated with the return to democratic rule.[20]

US restrictions on nuclear commerce also played a role in impeding the nuclear programmes of Brazil and Argentina in the 1980s, partly to counteract the deals they had made with Germany and France. In an attempt to slow the development of nuclear-weapons capability, Washington blocked Brazil's access to high-speed computers and other advanced technologies. Similar restrictions were imposed on Argentina. The United States also impeded Brazil's access to much-needed loans from international financial institutions.

Reiss contends that these measures 'increased the amount of time needed to complete projects and raised their costs ... The examples of Argentina and Brazil strongly suggest that export controls can make a significant difference in preventing countries from increasing their nuclear competence.'[21] José Goldemberg, Brazil's former secretary of state for science and technology, argues that external efforts to hold back the nuclear programmes of Argentina and Brazil 'fell flat', although he acknowledges that because of these restrictions the nuclear programmes moved ahead more slowly.[22] Neither country was persuaded by sanctions to abandon nuclear-weapons development, but external restrictions made it more difficult to obtain the technologies and materials needed in their nascent programmes. As the costs increased in comparison to the expected benefits, political leaders decided to abandon weapons development. They did so more on the basis of domestic political considerations than in response to external pressures.

Newly elected civilian presidents were strongly nationalist but were also able to build momentum to improve bilateral political relations. Both governments realised the political and commercial benefits of joining the NPT. Similarly, civilian leaders recognised that military dreams of grandeur did not serve the national interest. Goldemberg writes that he and others convinced Brazilian President Fernando Collor de Mello that 'the road to enter the First World is not the development of nuclear weapons but solving the problems of underdevelopment'.[23] Argentina was willing to join Brazil in this approach, and the two sides signed a series of agreements in 1991 that committed them to the renunciation of nuclear weapons, including the signing of the Treaty of Tlatelolco. They also established a joint organisation, the Brazilian–Argentine Agency for Accounting and Control of Nuclear Materials (ABACC), to conduct mutual inspections of nuclear facilities and reassure each other of good-faith compliance.

The example of Argentina and Brazil strongly suggests, according to Reiss, that 'resolution, or at least amelioration, of outstanding political disagreements must precede cooperation in the nuclear sphere'.[24] This is an important but sobering lesson for addressing proliferation challenges elsewhere. It will be necessary to resolve fundamental political disputes between India and Pakistan and between Israel and its Arab neighbours, for example, to eliminate nuclear weapons in these regions.

Lessons from South Africa

The end of the South African nuclear programme in 1990 resulted from a change in the country's security environment and a decisive shift in domestic political governance. The programme had been justified as a response to the presumed communist threat from Cuban troops and Marxist adversaries in neighbouring countries, all backed by the Soviet Union. It was also a response to growing isolation and international opposition to the regime's apartheid policies. When these internal and external conditions changed, induced in part through international pressure against apartheid, the justifications for retaining nuclear weapons disappeared. For many South African leaders, the removal of external dangers obviated the need for nuclear weapons.

South Africa's international isolation negatively influenced decisions about its nuclear programme. International ostracism intensified the government's siege mentality, which played a role in the initial decision to develop nuclear weapons. The government's isolation also reinforced the parochial world view of the Afrikaner leadership, which rarely travelled outside the country. These factors contributed to an air of unreality in the decision-making of top government officials. Their decision to build nuclear weapons as a means to bolster the regime's security was likened by one senior official to 'building castles in the air'.[25]

The security situation changed abruptly with the fall of the Berlin Wall and global collapse of communism. Even more important was the tripartite agreement concluded in December 1989 between South Africa, Angola and Cuba for the withdrawal of Cuban forces from Angola. In announcing the decision to dismantle the nuclear programme, South African President F.W. de Klerk emphasised the dramatic change in the country's security environment, especially the end of the Cold War and the removal of the presumed threat from regional communist forces. De Klerk specifically mentioned the withdrawal of Cuban forces from Angola and the independence of Namibia. It has also been noted that de Klerk also may have been motivated by a racially driven desire to keep nuclear weapons out of the hands of the leaders of the African National Congress.[26]

The political environment shifted profoundly when the anti-apartheid resistance movement forced the regime to yield power. When the South African government freed Nelson Mandela and opened a dialogue for political transition, it also issued orders to terminate the nuclear programme and dismantle the country's six nuclear devices. This was followed in 1991 by the signing of a comprehensive safeguards agreement with the IAEA and South Africa's accession to the NPT.

The decision to end the nuclear programme was motivated primarily by political considerations. Powerful voices within the apartheid establishment had never favoured the development of nuclear weapons, believing correctly that they exacerbated tensions with the United States and European countries and frustrated long-term efforts to integrate with the West. The continued presence of nuclear weapons was a barrier to joining the NPT and thereby gaining valuable access to peaceful nuclear technology and international cooperation on nuclear-energy development. Close cooperation in nuclear matters with Israel did not help to improve the international reputation of the apartheid regime.

As de Klerk acknowledged: 'A nuclear deterrent had become not only superfluous but in fact an obstacle to the development of South Africa's international relations'.[27] The United States and other Western governments were strenuously opposed to South Africa's nuclear programme. In the late 1970s they pressured Pretoria to abandon efforts to test a nuclear device in the Kalahari Desert after Soviet satellites detected preparation for the test.

South Africa's decision to empower the African majority and disavow nuclear weapons has burnished South Africa's image and stature regionally and internationally. As the only state to have dismantled indigenously produced nuclear weapons voluntarily, South Africa has unique moral authority in advocating global disarmament and criticising the remaining nuclear weapons states for their inaction in fulfilling nuclear-disarmament obligations under Article VI of the NPT.

Libya comes clean

In December 2003 Libyan leader Muammar Gadhafi surprised many observers by announcing his government's decision to disclose and dismantle its nuclear-, chemical- and biological-weapons programmes and to allow international inspectors to verify compliance. Gadhafi had started his quest for nuclear weapons soon after he came to power through a military coup in 1969. His government's ratification of the NPT in 1975 had no effect in restraining Libyan efforts to buy a bomb from one of the emerging NWS, and later to assemble technology and fissile material to construct an indigenous bomb. When Libya gave up its weapons programme in 2003 US officials claimed the decision was due to what one US congressman termed the 'pedagogic value' of the invasion of Iraq.[28] In reality, though, Libya's abandonment of its weapons programme had little to do with the war in Iraq. Its decision was rooted in a process of diplomatic engagement, facilitated by a deft combination of sanctions and incentives, dating back more than a decade to the successful US and UN diplomatic effort in the 1990s to dissuade Libya from supporting international terrorism.

In her recent book on non-proliferation norms, Maria Rost Rublee agrees that the fear of regime change was not the key reason for giving up the bomb. Neither were economic sanctions per se. By the end of the 1990s, with the lifting of UN sanctions, European countries started to relax their restrictions on trade with Libya, which made it easier for Tripoli to tolerate unilateral US sanctions that had been initiated in 1986. Rublee stresses that while sanctions mattered in the decision to renounce WMD, more important was Gadhafi's commitment, made under pressure from a domestic reformist and pragmatist constituency, to transform Libya into a growing modern country ready to reassert regional leadership. The quest for WMD capabilities and consequent economic sanctions stood in the way of this ambition.[29]

Libya's decision to abandon weapons development grew also out of its choice to end its policy of state sponsorship of terrorism. In this case, the dismantlement of nuclear weapons is linked to the prevention of global terrorism. It highlights the deadly nexus of proliferation and terrorism at the top of the international security agenda, and shows that sanctions and incentives can be combined effectively as instruments of bargaining leverage to change the behaviour of a previously recalcitrant government. The immediate catalyst for Gadhafi's decision was the US- and British-led interdiction in 2003 of a German-registered ship heading for Libya, which was carrying equipment that could be used to develop centrifuges. This operation exemplified the US-led Proliferation Security Initiative (PSI) and was an important success in demonstrating the effectiveness of multilateral naval cooperation to prevent weapons trafficking.

In the years preceding the imposition of the UN sanctions in 1992, Libya was implicated in the bombings of Pan Am Flight 103 in 1988 and French flight UTA 772 in 1989. After sanctions were imposed for terrorist support and activity, Libya ceased its attacks against international aviation, prompting the US State Department's 1996 report on global terrorism to note: 'Terrorism by Libya has been sharply reduced by UN sanctions'.[30]

Targeted UN sanctions did not cause major economic disruption in Libya, but they isolated the regime and provided sufficient leverage to prompt a reconsideration of policy and a diplomatic settlement of the Pan Am bombing case. In 1998 Libya agreed to turn over suspects wanted in connection with the airline bombing to an international tribunal in The Hague. The Security Council responded by suspending and later lifting sanctions. The United States maintained its sanctions, however, demanding that Tripoli take further steps to compensate the victims of terrorist attacks and cooperate in counter-terrorism and non-proliferation efforts. Through a series of complex negotiations, US officials made clear that sanctions could be lifted and commercial relations with the West opened if Libya would agree to dismantle its weapons programmes. Libya had tried to start negotiations several times in the course of the 1990s, but Washington insisted it would not engage until Tripoli renounced its WMD plans.

Libya's decision to comply with Western demands was motivated primarily by its desire to escape isolation and gain access to Western markets and technology. According to Flynt Leverett, former senior director for Middle Eastern affairs at the US National Security Council: 'Libya was willing to deal because of credible diplomatic representations ... that doing so was critical to achieving their strategic and domestic goals'.[31] Former Assistant Secretary of State Thomas E. McNamara, who was responsible for US policy towards Libya during the earlier years, attributed Gadhafi's turnaround to the long-term effects of sanctions, the successful interdiction of the weapons shipment at sea, and the accumulated impact of years of diplomatic pressure and dialogue.[32] Incentives were crucial factors in persuading Libya to abandon its nuclear-weapons programme.

Ukraine gives up the bomb

Economic incentives and security assurances also played a role in persuading Ukraine to give up the nuclear weapons on its soil that it inherited with the collapse of the Soviet Union. Faced with disastrous economic conditions and seeking economic and political independence from Russia, Ukrainian officials traded away the nuclear weapons for economic and security benefits. The result was the January 1994 Trilateral Statement, signed by the presidents of Ukraine, the United States and Russia, in which the United States promised substantial economic assistance and support for greater Ukrainian integration into Western financial and security institutions, while Russia, the United States and the United Kingdom offered assurances for Ukraine's security. The Ukrainian military supported the decision to remove nuclear weapons because their maintenance would have swallowed a major part of its military budget that could now be used to strengthen conventional forces.[33] In January 1996 Ukraine became a non-nuclear nation when the transfer of 4,400 warheads to Russia was completed.

The Trilateral Statement followed the 1992 Lisbon Protocol, in which Russia, Belarus, Kazakhstan and Ukraine agreed to become parties to the Strategic Arms Reduction Treaty (START) and the Nuclear Non-Proliferation Treaty. Before ratifying START, however, the Ukrainian Parliament announced in late 1993 a set of conditions for its approval. These stated that Ukraine would dismantle only 42% of its warheads, and only after receiving security assurances from the United States and Russia. Presidents Bill Clinton and Boris Yeltsin immediately engaged in further negotiations with Ukrainian President Leonid Kravchuk. In the resulting Trilateral Statement agreement the United States and other countries provided Ukraine substantial financial assistance in exchange for the removal of all nuclear warheads from missiles and their transference to Russia. Washington pledged more than $900 million in Nunn–Lugar funds under the Cooperative Threat Reduction Programme and other assistance programmes. Russia offered to write off more than $2 billion of Ukrainian oil and gas debts. Russia also pledged to blend down the highly enriched uranium extracted from returned nuclear warheads and return it to Ukraine as reactor fuel for nuclear power generation. The European Union and individual European states collectively contributed hundreds of millions of dollars in related nuclear assistance to the former Soviet republics.

All of these efforts combined to provide very substantial economic assistance and encouragement for denuclearisation. Similar offers of assistance were provided to Kazakhstan and Belarus to encourage these former Soviet states to give up the nuclear weapons on their soil as well. Because of financial and economic benefits 'it literally became profitable' for Ukraine, Kazakhstan and Belarus to renounce nuclear weapons.[34] The provision of financial assistance was intended to demonstrate a commitment to the political independence and economic viability of the former Soviet republics, based on sustained relationships of cooperation with the West and Russia.

In addition to financial assistance, the United States, Russia and other countries provided explicit security guarantees to Ukraine upon its accession to the NPT. In December 1994, at a summit of the Commission on Security and Cooperation in Europe (CSCE), the United States, Russia and the United Kingdom provided Ukraine with formal negative and positive security assurances, pledging not to use nuclear weapons against it, to respect its political and economic sovereignty and to provide assistance should Ukraine fall victim to a nuclear attack. France gave its own formal assurances to Ukraine unilaterally at the summit.

Security assurances played an important role in the successful denuclearisation of Ukraine. These guarantees supported Ukraine as a sovereign and legitimate member of the international community. By possessing nuclear weapons it might have become a pariah state. For Ukraine's leaders the nuclear weapons on its soil were not means of security but high-value bargaining chips that were used to obtain what the newly independent country needed most: economic assistance and political cooperation from the West, and national autonomy and security assurances vis-à-vis Russia. Kiev traded 'essentially unusable nuclear weapons for a set of relationships, especially with Washington, that would help ensure the country's future'.[35]

By giving up the nuclear weapons, Ukraine realised its most urgent national objectives: political recognition, territorial security and economic assistance. The United States and its allies achieved their objectives as well: preventing the emergence of a new nuclear-weapons state and the further proliferation of nuclear weapons.

Conclusion

These cases show that national decisions to forgo the nuclear option cannot be explained by any single factor. Democratic transitions obviously helped political leaders see the world with new eyes. This happened in Argentina and Brazil, which developed a new atmosphere of mutual trust and transparency, and in South Africa, which abandoned old prejudices and ended apartheid. For Pretoria the decision to dismantle nuclear weapons was facilitated by a drastic change in the security environment. For Ukraine security guarantees were an important factor in encouraging denuclearisation. Incentives from the United States and other states encouraged this process.

Economic sanctions alone are not enough to alter a government's policies, even though they may have major negative impacts. More important, as both the Libyan and South African cases reaffirm, is the realisation by governments that ending political and economic isolation may bring positive long-term benefits. The calculation of future prospects finds nuclear weapons to be a liability rather than an asset. Skilful international responses that combine incentives and penalties can shape that judgement.

CHAPTER FOUR

Lessons from the End of the Cold War

The way in which the Cold War ended illustrates the essential relationship between improved political relations and disarmament. It shows that conciliatory gestures can help to improve political relations and generate a pattern of positive reciprocity leading to sharp reductions in weapons levels and enhanced overall security. It confirms the value of arms-control negotiations as a framework for improving political relations and reducing arsenals. This lesson came late to the leading nuclear weapons states, which became seriously involved in arms control only when the arms race began to spiral out of control and after the terrifying brush with catastrophe during the Cuban missile crisis. Disaster was averted more by luck than design. The nuclear age has been rife with other accidents and close calls.[1]

Ultimately, however, the Cold War was brought to an end through political processes and economic pressure. Several institutions, policies and strategies played a role in the historic transformation of the Soviet Union. Perhaps chief among these were arms-control negotiation, the influence of the evolving concept of common security and the links between nuclear and conventional disarmament. Initiatives by Gorbachev sparked the great changes of the late 1980s, but the roots of the process can be traced to earlier periods of détente, when arms control and confidence-building measures established a foundation for future cooperation. Gorbachev's concessions finally broke the ice and opened the way to dramatic arms reduction and improvement in East–West relations. The pendulum has swung in the other direction in recent years, as tensions between Russia and the West have risen, but the basic lessons of that era remain valid. Initiatives for tension reduction can establish patterns of positive reciprocity that enhance security and reduce reliance on nuclear weapons.

The arms control framework

Disarmament is both a precondition for and consequence of cooperative relationships among the great powers.[2] Hans Morgenthau wrote that 'disarmament contributes to the improvement of the political situation by lessening political tensions and by creating confidence in the purposes of the respective nations'.[3] Disarmament diplomacy can help to facilitate great-power cooperation, which in turn can improve political relations and make further disarmament possible. Yet the end of the Cold War did not fulfill the promise of sustained improvement in East–West political relations. Old competing interests and prejudices die slowly and the institutional framework for cooperation remained imperfect and contested.

Between the 1970s and the 1990s, the formal agreements that brought about arms reductions were adopted within the framework of traditional arms-control negotiations. The Intermediate-Range Nuclear Forces (INF) and START treaties provided a legal framework within which the United States and the Soviet Union could reach accommodation. Throughout the Cold War era, the structures of arms control offered a context to assure stability in an otherwise tense atmosphere of nuclear-arms competition. Even when the negotiations produced little or no progress in arms restraint, they created channels of communication and provided predictability in a high-stakes setting. This in itself was an important contribution to security. In the latter part of the 1980s the arms control framework provided the setting in which Gorbachev's revolutionary initiatives could break through to reduce political tensions and lower weapons levels.

The immediate events that brought an end to the Cold War were sparked by independent initiatives and political concessions by Gorbachev. In August 1985, on the 40th anniversary of the Hiroshima bombing, the Soviet leader unilaterally ordered a halt to Soviet underground nuclear testing and urged the United States to follow suit. Gorbachev also announced sweeping transformations in Soviet security policy and proposed deep cuts in nuclear weapons.

Reykjavík was the turning point. Gorbachev and Reagan seemed to compete with each other in proposals on how deeply to cut nuclear arsenals. They came close to agreeing on the elimination of all nuclear weapons, although the deal foundered over differences on missile defence. Reagan was slow to respond to Gorbachev's gestures, but in 1987, when the Soviet leader accepted deep cuts without restrictions on missile defence, Washington said 'yes' to Moscow's 'da'. Dramatic arms reductions that few would have considered conceivable a few years earlier followed in rapid succession.

Common security

Gorbachev was motivated in part by the principles of common security, which were first articulated in the 1982 report of the Independent Commission on Disarmament and Security Issues, chaired by Swedish Prime Minister Olof Palme, entitled

Common Security. The report proposed a new framework for international security and offered strategies for reversing the nuclear arms race through East–West negotiations. The work of the Palme Commission was prompted by tense political relations between the Soviet Union and the United States, during a time of action–reaction missile deployments in Europe and growing public fear of nuclear war on the continent.[4]

The concept of common security captured a fundamental truth of international politics: that the security of one nation cannot be gained at the expense of others. The competitive deployment of nuclear and conventional weapons, especially if they are perceived to serve aggressive purposes, becomes a source of tensions. Offensive build-ups affect not only the rival but also the initiating party, raising insecurities on both sides. The dilemma can be remedied only by mutual restraint and cooperation.

Common security principles transcend the narrow limits of political realism. In the realist paradigm all states face a security dilemma, are locked in a continuous struggle for power in a competitive system of international relations, and are forced to rely on self-help to protect and enhance their power. This competition for power is linked to the competition for arms. As Morgenthau emphasised, 'a mutually satisfactory settlement of the competition for power is a precondition for disarmament'.[5] Nations will not reduce their reliance on weapons if they fear for their security and are threatened by neighbours. The security dilemma has a flip side, however. When nations build weapons to reduce their own vulnerabilities, they may create vulnerabilities and insecurities in others. When a state seeks to accumulate military power for its own security, it may alter the strategic balance and reduce the security of other states. Morgenthau stated that 'the armaments race aggravates the struggle for power through the fear it generates and the burdens it imposes'.[6] These positive and negative security dynamics are unavoidable. The essential insight of common security is that states cannot increase their own security by diminishing that of others. The greatest security is obtained through a mutual balancing of interests and the enhancement of cooperation.

Systems of arms control and disarmament are attempts to transcend the dilemmas and contradictions of the competition for security. Arms reduction agreements represent 'a daring bet on an alternative security policy', in the words of Müller. They embody principles of security that are shaped by international cooperation, the rule of law, self-restraint and mutual confidence.[7] They assert that cooperative security arrangements have a legitimate place in international relations.

The security dilemma persists, however. What is rational for the whole may not be perceived as compelling for the individual. Renouncing the most powerful weapons seems inherently contradictory to the basic impulses of state security, a leap into unfamiliar terrain, a fateful decision that may be perceived as increasing national vulnerability.[8]

The power of positive reciprocity

Gorbachev's initiatives affirmed the principles of positive reciprocity. Cooperation theorists have demonstrated through game theory experiments that mutually beneficial gestures of cooperation can generate, in specific conditions, patterns of positive reciprocity. Alexander Wendt observed that positive reciprocation can foster a sense of common identification and help to create mutual interests between former adversaries.[9] At a basic level, conciliatory action is useful as a way of reducing distrust and establishing the foundations for cooperative behaviour.[10]

The history of the Cold War confirms the value of conciliatory gestures as means of encouraging positive reciprocity and inducing cooperative behaviour. In relations between the United States and the Soviet Union, conciliatory gestures often led to reduced tensions, while hardline policies usually produced a mirror response of heightened animosity. Charles Osgood, Amitai Etzioni and others have developed models of how positive reciprocity helps to reduce tensions between adversaries.[11] A state can make unilateral initiatives for reciprocity, because in the case of a failure it is always possible to return to the status quo ante without sacrificing anything irreparable. Gorbachev's actions seemed to be an enactment of this strategy, to which the Reagan administration responded.

Perhaps the most significant illustration of the power of positive reciprocity for disarmament occurred with the Presidential Nuclear Initiatives (PNI). In this instance Washington took the lead, and the Soviet response was immediate. The PNI process began in September 1991 when President George H.W. Bush announced the unilateral demobilisation of US tactical nuclear weapons from ships and submarines and the removal and dismantling of nuclear artillery and short-range missiles in Europe. He also lowered the alert status of all US strategic bombers and Inter-Continental Ballistic Missiles (ICBMs) slated for deactivation under the START agreement. Gorbachev promptly reciprocated, announcing a similar withdrawal and dismantling of many tactical nuclear weapons from Soviet land forces and naval vessels and the de-alerting of strategic forces.

These reciprocal independent reductions resulted in the largest single act of denuclearisation in history, removing as many as 17,000 nuclear weapons from deployment.[12] They were carried out without controversy or major opposition in either country and seemed at the time a natural and logical consequence of the new post-Cold War era in which political relationships were improved and vast arsenals of tactical nuclear weapons were regarded as a dangerous liability rather than a source of security.

Nuclear disarmament and enhanced conventional security

Some fear that the elimination of nuclear weapons would make the world safe for world war and spark conventional arms races.[13] History teaches that the reverse is more likely. Disarmament is tied to processes of improved political relations and arms reductions that make war less likely. Immediately after the Cold War, in the 1990s, nuclear arms reductions were linked to lower proliferation dangers, cuts in conventional force levels and a greater reliance on the United Nations to address security challenges and resolve armed conflicts.

Yet the process of reciprocity is neither linear nor predictable. It can have asymmetries, discontinuities and gaps that interrupt cooperation dynamics before they can gather sustainable momentum. The opponents of arms-reduction policies can manipulate them for their own political purposes and criticise decision-makers for neglecting national interests. This happened both in Russia and the United States in the 2000s when President Vladimir Putin reversed Boris Yeltsin's weak and disorganised foreign policies and the Bush administration opted for military primacy and unilateralism. It is remarkable, though, that despite tense political relations, neither Moscow nor Washington took major steps towards rearmament; with the exception of the Anti-Ballistic Missile Treaty and the Conventional Forces in Europe (CFE) Treaty, both sides have continued to respect existing arms control treaties. The cooperative spirit of the immediate post-Cold War era has frayed but seems to have some staying power.

The relationship between the control of nuclear and conventional arms in Europe has been a complex one. East–West détente in the early 1970s led to the creation of the Conference on Security and Cooperation in Europe (CSCE) and culminated in the Helsinki Final Act in 1975. The main purpose of the Act was to define and establish the status quo in Europe and to agree on basic principles concerning political relations, economic interaction and human rights. NATO pressed for a two-track approach in which the Helsinki process would be complemented by the control of conventional arms. For this purpose Mutual and Balanced Force Reduction (MBFR) talks were started in 1973.

The talks were intended to place limits on Soviet conventional forces, which at that time were considered superior to NATO forces. While not directly connected with the process of strategic arms control, the talks had relevance for NATO's nuclear doctrine: the more constrained Warsaw Pact forces were, the less likely it was that NATO would have to resort to the doctrine of flexible response, which would mean the deployment of more nuclear weapons in Europe (which European states both demanded and detested). In that sense, the MBFR talks helped to maintain the internal cohesion of the NATO Alliance.

Both the Helsinki and the MBFR processes were affected by the state of East–West relations. When the 'second Cold War' started in the late 1970s, talks on conventional arms stalled. With the arrival of Gorbachev and the easing of political tensions in the mid-1980s, new nuclear and conventional disarmament agreements followed. The INF and START agreements that helped to bring an end to the Cold War were paralleled by negotiations for the CFE Treaty that reduced conventional force levels in Europe.

The foundations for the arms-reduction agreements and mutual security assurances that facilitated the end of the Cold War were established in the 1986 Stockholm Agreement between NATO and the Warsaw Pact. The agreement was designed to reduce the risk of military confrontation in Europe and to 'give expression to the duty of states to refrain from the threat or use of force in their mutual relations as well as in their international relations in general'.[14] It also contained significant confidence- and security-building measures, which provided for prior notification and on-site inspection of any massing of military forces or large-scale military exercises.

The agreement showed, Gorbachev declared at the time, 'that even in a complex situation it is possible to reach agreement on questions of security if there is the political will and desire'.[15] The on-site inspection provisions were particularly crucial. They carried over into the subsequent CFE and START treaties and proved to be crucial elements of the increased mutual confidence and rapprochement that led to the end of the Cold War.

The CFE Treaty entered into force in 1990. Widely considered a cornerstone of European security and a central element of European stability, it is a highly comprehensive arms-control regime that establishes limits on the numbers of tanks, armoured combat vehicles, heavy artillery, combat aircraft and attack helicopters that NATO countries and Russia and its former republics can deploy between the Atlantic Ocean and the Ural Mountains. The treaty includes a range of confidence-building and transparency measures, including on-site inspections. The parties to the treaty have carried out more than 5,000 routine and challenge on-site inspections.[16]

The treaty originally contained language limiting weapons by blocs and zones, but this was replaced in the Adapted CFE Treaty of 1999 with national and territorial arms ceilings. In recent years the treaty has faced severe challenges as political relations between Russia and the West have deteriorated. Some NATO countries have refused to ratify it because, in their view, Russia has not complied with its provisions. Moscow has not carried out the required withdrawal of troops and weaponry from Moldova and Georgia. Russia is today so deeply engaged in the Northern Caucasus that the old CFE Treaty would constrain its policy options and military actions.

In July 2007 President Putin announced Russia was suspending its implementation of the CFE treaty, including on-site inspections. In doing so Moscow invoked the 'extraordinary circumstances' stipulation in the treaty. These circumstances included Western support for Georgia and the planning of missile-defence sites in the Czech Republic and Poland. Russia is seeking to reassert its international and regional geopolitical status and finds the limitations of CFE unacceptable. It considers that the treaty's ceilings on heavy weapons, its requirements for on-site inspections and the issue of possible NATO membership for Georgia and Ukraine are all inconsistent with Russian security objectives.

Conclusion

The end of the Cold War in Europe hastened the collapse of the bipolar world order and alleviated the structural and political rivalry on the continent. The construction of a new security regime since the late 1960s had a decisive impact on the peaceful nature of this transformation. Agreement between the opponents on key political principles, reciprocal patterns of cooperation, treaties on nuclear and conventional arms control, institutional arrangements and the emphasis on human rights and democracy all contributed to Europe becoming 'whole and free' without any significant prospect of violence.[17]

If the peaceful resolution to the division of Europe has any lessons for other regions, they concern the importance of regime formation in which norms and institutions are established on political, security and humanitarian issues. Such regimes cannot solve all problems, but they help to absorb conflict potential and provide institutional means to transform and settle disputes. In the context of nuclear disarmament this means that the myriad political tensions and conflicts that appear between competing states and other actors need not escalate into armed confrontations, but can be contained on the basis of minimal common values and interests.

The transition towards improved security relationships is seldom smooth. The weakness of Russia after the collapse of the Soviet Union created an asymmetry that many in Moscow resented but were unable to alter. The West pursued mostly pragmatic policies, but strains of triumphalism were also in the air. The economic recovery of Russia after the financial meltdown in 1998 and the rise of new political leaders created discontinuities between the old and the new.

Russian foreign policy under Putin seeks to do away with political and military asymmetries, although in a manner that is not fully acceptable to the West. A critical concern is that Russia seems to consider its strategic and tactical nuclear weapons essential elements of a new symmetry and thus may be unwilling to reduce them towards zero. If Russia remains addicted to nuclear weapons, as are many in the West, the road to nuclear abolition will be much rockier.

CHAPTER FIVE

Assuring Security

Security concerns are the primary factors explaining why states choose to acquire or relinquish nuclear weapons. These concerns are mediated through domestic political debates and can be significantly influenced by external incentives or disincentives, but they are fundamentally about perceptions of state security and national interest. It follows from this that any systematic process of disarmament must prioritise security concerns. States choosing not to acquire the bomb must have credible assurances that they will be protected against nuclear attack and will not be subject to aggression or intimidation by other states. Nations relinquishing the bomb need viable alternative means of maintaining and enhancing their power.

Different types of security assurances have played a role in winning political support for non-proliferation. Pledges not to use nuclear weapons against non-nuclear states have been devalued over the years as the major powers developed new, enlarged missions for these weapons. Nuclear weapons have become more important to security planners, contrary to official declarations of support for nuclear abolition. US pledges of extended deterrence are essential elements of security planning among allies in Europe and East Asia. These vows to use nuclear weapons if necessary are partly directed at Russia and China, which makes it difficult to establish relations of trust and cooperation among the three powers. In this context nuclear-deterrence pledges have become less credible, and they contradict the negative security assurances that were part of the agreement extending the NPT. Alternative security strategies can provide protection at less risk and lower cost.

Assurances

Security assurances are of two types, positive and negative. Positive assurances are pledges to come to the assistance of states that are threatened by nuclear attack. Negative assurances are pledges not to use nuclear weapons under specified conditions against states without these weapons. The most common form of security assurance is the pledge by the nuclear-weapons states not to use nuclear weapons against state parties to the NPT. Negative assurances have proven to be very important to building confidence in and support for non-proliferation. Both positive and negative assurances are based on the collective security pledges of the UN Charter not to use military force against other member states and to come to their defence if they are attacked.

Security assurances were included in UN Security Council resolutions in 1968 when negotiations for the NPT were concluded, and in 1995 when the treaty was indefinitely extended. Resolution 1887, which was adopted in September 2009 by heads of states in session at the Security Council, reaffirmed the importance of these security assurances as means of strengthening the Treaty.[1]

Positive assurances were offered in 1968. The Security Council adopted Resolution 255 recognising that 'certain states' (the United States, the Soviet Union and the United Kingdom) pledged to provide immediate assistance to any non-nuclear-weapons country that might be attacked or threatened by such weapons.[2] China and France did not join in this pledge. The relevance of the resolution was diminished by the fact that the NWS were not prepared to act in unison on the question. The resolution was nonetheless important as a concession by the three nuclear-armed signatories to win support for the treaty among non-nuclear weapons states.

In 1995 negative security assurances were provided, again as part of a diplomatic package to gain political support for the NPT, this time for indefinite extension. Resolution 984 noted 'with appreciation the statements made by each of the nuclear-weapon states' providing assurances against nuclear attack.[3] These security guarantees were qualified, however, and they identified options and exceptions where nuclear weapons might be used. Russia stated that only non-nuclear weapons states that did not have nuclear weapons on their soil would be provided assurances. This meant that countries such as Germany, Turkey and the Netherlands, with US nuclear weapons on their soil under NATO authority, could be targeted. NATO member states limited their non-nuclear pledges to states not allied with a nuclear-weapons state. This meant that Belarus could face nuclear threats if it joined a Russian attack. Only China offered an unequivocal and unconditional pledge not to attack a non-nuclear state with nuclear weapons.

Security assurances also exist in treaties establishing nuclear weapons-free zones. In the protocols to the nuclear-free treaties for Latin America, Africa, the South Pacific, Southeast Asia and Central Asia, the nuclear-weapons states pledge not to attack or threaten members of the zone. The United States, the United Kingdom and France have not signed the Central Asian treaty because of a clause stating that existing treaty commitments are not overruled, which implies the possibility of Russia introducing nuclear weapons on to the territory of its allies in the region.

In recent years, as nuclear weapons have assumed more expansive missions beyond deterrence, security assurances have been downgraded in importance. They have received less political support and have become matters of lower priority to the major powers. Nonetheless, negative security assurances remain significant in gaining the confidence and support of non-nuclear states for strengthened international non-proliferation controls. It is noteworthy that assurances were issued at precisely the most important historical moments when the NPT was initially approved and when it was indefinitely extended. This confirms the link between security assurances and non-proliferation. Negative security assurances were important elements of successful diplomatic efforts in the early 1990s to dissuade Ukraine and Kazakhstan from maintaining former Soviet nuclear weapons on their soil.

Stretching deterrence

The original justification for nuclear weapons was to deter nuclear attack from another country, but over the years the US nuclear mission broadened to include the defence of key allies in Europe and Asia. This happened in the 1950s and 1960s when the United States replaced the doctrine of massive retaliation with flexible response and extended deterrence. Since then US policy has been based on the promise to come to the aid of allies with the use of nuclear weapons if necessary. This is a first use policy, a pledge to use nuclear weapons to counter nuclear or conventional attack against allies. The nuclear umbrella continues to be an essential element of security planning in Europe and Asia. Its removal, critics charge, will result in a cascade of nuclear proliferation, with nations scrambling to acquire their own nuclear-deterrent capability.

The 'new nuclear debate' – as deputy-head of the NATO Secretary-General's policy planning unit Michael Rühle calls the recent initiatives on nuclear disarmament – poses a major challenge to the alliance's policy. NATO is a nuclear alliance in which the deployment of tactical nuclear weapons in Europe, so-called 'nuclear sharing', plays a central role. Since ending shared deterrence will not help to stem proliferation, Rühle argues, 'arms control delusions' should be buried. In this view, nuclear weapons continue to serve a useful part in NATO's deterrence strategy and should be retained to avoid internal frictions within the alliance.[4] Most NATO states, especially the new members from the East, are keen to receive credible pledges from the United States under Article V of the North Atlantic Charter on the defence of their territories in the event of an attack, presumably by Russia. In Germany, however, officials have called for removing US tactical nuclear weapons from their soil.

The debate over extended deterrence has intensified recently in Japan. The electoral victory of the Democratic Party of Japan (DPJ) in August 2009 changed the debate on disarmament and extended deterrence. The declared policy of the DPJ is no first use and the doctrine of 'sole purpose', which states that nuclear weapons should serve only to deter other nuclear weapons. Katsuya Okada, Japan's foreign minister and former secretary-general of the DPJ, has been a staunch advocate of this stance, although bureaucrats and experts in the Japanese government have resisted the idea in favour of the continuation of the traditional policy of extended deterrence. Okada told a session of the Diet in May that 'a norm not allowing at least first use, or making it illegal to use nuclear weapons against countries not possessing nuclear weapons, should be established'. Former US Secretary of Defense William Perry called on the new government at a Tokyo press conference in October 2009 to adopt the sole purpose stand.[5] The independent commission that looks into the role of the IAEA also recommended in 2008 that nuclear-weapons countries 'should clearly state that nuclear weapons have no purpose except to deter attacks by nuclear weapons'.[6]

Alternative deterrence options are available. The conventional force balance for self-defence favours Japan and allied American forces and provides a credible security alternative to nuclear deterrence. Japanese security is well protected by its relatively small but very capable Self Defense Forces and by strong backing from the United States. China and North Korea have very large armed forces but cannot match the modern, technologically advanced weaponry available to the United States and its Japanese and South Korean allies. The naval balance, which would be critical to the defence of Japan, especially favours the United States and its allies. The US–Japan security treaty remains in effect and would become even more important in a non-nuclear world. The conventional force capabilities available to Japan provide protection against potential military attack and are a more credible deterrent than the threat to use nuclear weapons.

Scott Sagan has argued that the term 'nuclear umbrella' is highly misleading and should be dropped from the strategic lexicon. The term implies a degree of protection that does not actually exist, and blurs the distinction between deterrence against nuclear-armed states and the broader concept of deterrence against other non-nuclear security threats. Focusing on the former would amount to a no first use policy. This would allow a shift in deterrence strategy to emphasise conventional responses to conventional threats. If conventional-force threats were to increase, nations could respond either by attempting to negotiate mutual constraints or if necessary by increasing their own conventional capabilities. A conventional protection strategy would be credible militarily and would avoid the dilemma caused by uncertainty about the willingness of the US to use nuclear weapons when its own security is not directly jeopardised.[7]

Doubts about nuclear deterrence

A dose of realism is needed about the claims that are made on behalf of nuclear deterrence. Undoubtedly the presence of nuclear weapons makes the leaders of nuclear-armed nations more cautious about directly confronting one another militarily. This does not mean, however, that nuclear deterrence has prevented war in the past or will do so in the future. These are untestable propositions in any case. Nuclear deterrence during the Cold War did not prevent so-called limited wars in Korea, Vietnam and Afghanistan that took millions of lives. Nor was it necessarily the decisive factor in preventing war between the great powers. Political scientist John Vasquez has emphasised that many other factors beyond the presence of nuclear weapons accounted for the 'long peace' that prevailed after the Second World War.[8] International relations scholar John Lewis Gaddis argues that nuclear weapons induced some degree of caution in East–West relations but were not the sole nor even the primary factors accounting for the absence of war between the United States and the Soviet Union.[9] A recent analysis by non-proliferation scholar Ward Wilson finds that 'the practical record of nuclear deterrence shows doubtful successes and proven failures'.[10]

Doubts about the viability of nuclear deterrence increase in an era of greater multipolarity and the diffusion of nuclear threats. Deterrence becomes more uncertain in triadic relationships and in complex coalitional arrangements. There is no evidence that states make decisions to acquire or relinquish nuclear weapons primarily on the basis of great-power deterrence. Many question the relevance of nuclear deterrence in responding to terrorist strikes or possible nuclear acquisition by non-state actors: retaliation is impossible if enemies cannot be located and are prepared to die for their cause.

The diminishing credibility of nuclear deterrence prompts the search for alternatives. Replacing the doctrine of extended deterrence will require identifying and bolstering credible non-nuclear mechanisms for enhancing security. This can only be done in consultation with affected allies in Europe and East Asia through a process of collaborative analysis and policy consultation. George Perkovich has recommended cooperation with affected states and regions to evaluate regional security threats and define policy alternatives for addressing those challenges without nuclear weapons.[11] Non-nuclear security policies should be equal to or better than nuclear deterrence. The options for non-nuclear security include greater reliance on conventional defences, along with negotiated arms control and confidence-building measures, leading to more cooperative political relations and more active use of diplomatic incentives and pressures. Finding alternatives to extended nuclear deterrence and strengthening security assurances are essential for achieving disarmament.

No first use: reassurance for all

Security doctrines in Russia, the United States and other nuclear weapons states include the threat of possible first use of nuclear-weapons to deter conventional or other forms of attack from states and to counter the acquisition or use of nuclear, chemical or biological weapons by non-state actors. During the Cold War the Soviet Union adopted a declaratory policy of no first use, but in the 1990s, as its conventional military capabilities deteriorated, Russia abandoned this policy. The doctrine of possible deliberate first use of nuclear weapons has always been of dubious credibility: would the United States really initiate nuclear war to protect Taiwan or Latvia? Of course even a low probability of use provides some deterrent effect, but this prospect has become more uncertain over the years as the norm against nuclear-weapons use has strengthened. Any use of nuclear weapons contradicts the tenets of political realism. The initiating state would risk suffering a significant loss of status and global influence, not to mention its own devastation from potential retaliation.

The call for achieving a world without nuclear weapons has prompted renewed interest in the adoption of a universal no first use policy among nuclear-weapons states. Prominent experts have recommended that the nuclear-weapons states renew their negative security pledges and return to the original purpose of deterrence by vowing 'never to use or threaten to use nuclear weapons against states that do not have such weapons'.[12] This would be a major step towards limiting the role of these weapons and making it possible for states to proceed in a mutually balanced manner towards denuclearisation. If nuclear weapons have only the purpose of deterring attack from other nuclear-weapons states, a mutual process of disarmament becomes more feasible. As Sagan writes, nuclear-armed states 'could more easily coordinate moving in tandem to lower and equal levels of nuclear weapons on the road to zero'.[13] Universal negative security assurances through the commitment to no first use would be an important building block in constructing a nuclear weapons-free world.

Some analysts have urged that no first use pledges take the form of legally binding negative security assurances. The ultimate aim would be an international convention, or a new protocol to the NPT, in which all nuclear-weapons states join in providing comprehensive security assurances, perhaps adding their own specific reservations. The Weapons of Mass

Destruction Commission, chaired by Hans Blix, called for the inclusion of binding assurances by the nuclear weapons states as part of the NPT, and for the NWS outside the treaty to provide similar separate assurances.[14]

In the United States, there is ongoing debate regarding the merits of no first use assurances. The proposal has faced criticism from some US allies who fear the dilution of extended deterrence and a weakening of Washington's commitment to defend them in case of attack. Others have responded by pointing to the conventional military superiority of the United States, which would be more than sufficient against any military challenge to itself or allies.[15] Of course, the US conventional military interventions in Iraq and Afghanistan have not been unqualified successes. These are counter-insurgency wars, however, and are not the type of military engagement that is envisaged in the event of military threats against traditional US allies in Europe and East Asia. Against these kinds of threats US conventional power is well equipped and structured and provides a credible deterrent capability. Moreover, US power would likely be augmented by the contributions of allies if countries like South Korea or Poland were seriously threatened.

It is unlikely that the other nuclear-armed states (Israel, India, Pakistan and North Korea) would easily accept demands for no first use, since the *raison d'être* of their programmes is the threat to use their weapons as a last resort in the event of conventional attack. India has backed off from its previous commitment not to be the first to employ nuclear weapons.[16] Because of these obstacles, it may be better to start the process of developing negative security assurances in the context of bilateral and regional relations, for instance in South Asia. Mutual negative security pledges between China and India might begin to persuade Pakistan to back off from its long-held refusal to consider no first use, although such commitments in the nuclear realm would need to be accompanied by significant steps towards resolving deeply rooted geopolitical differences among the three states.

The big three

The key to achieving progress towards global disarmament is geostrategic cooperation among the great powers. Perkovich, Harald Müller and other analysts have emphasised the need for a 'concert of powers' in which the major nuclear weapons states – especially the United States, Russia and China – work together to resolve global conflicts and enhance cooperation, while moving steadily to reduce their reliance on nuclear weapons. Without such cooperation global nuclear disarmament is impossible.

The most important form of global security assurance is the forging of more cooperative political relationships among the three major powers. If the United States, Russia and China were able to work together more constructively, without threatening each other and while providing mutual security assurances, it would be much easier to extend a mantle of security assurance to other states and regions. As Perkovich writes: 'If relation ships among the US and Russia and China ... can be made more reassuring, more clearly defensive, then the pressure could be reduced on extended nuclear deterrence'.[17] The perceived need for nuclear umbrellas and strategic deterrence would diminish.

Of course, profound geopolitical differences exist among the United States, Russia and China. The three major states are engaged in a competition for power to protect and enlarge separately defined interests. In many respects this competition has intensified since the 1990s, and tensions among the states, especially between Russia and the United States, have increased. The basic reality of competing geopolitical interests will remain regardless of whether the states continue to rely on nuclear weapons. On the other hand, the big three are bound together in a delicate web of mutual inter-action to address common threats and interests. Nuclear non-proliferation is one of those concerns, and it leads to greater security cooperation.

All three of the major powers stand to gain from greater progress towards non-proliferation and disarmament. Each wants to preserve its position of regional and global influence, and would be threatened by destabilising or asymmetric power shifts. All agree on keeping nuclear weapons from pariah regimes or non-state actors. Each would benefit, although Russia less so, from diminishing the role of nuclear weapons in security policy. These common interests have generated cooperation among the big three in preventing proliferation in North Korea, countering the global threat from al-Qaeda and, to lesser degree, addressing the Iran dispute.

Greater cooperation among the three powers is an imperative for realising progress on non-proliferation and disarmament. Perkovich's comments on this matter underline what is at stake should the present efforts at internationalism fail:

> If relationships between the US and Russia and the US and China do not become much more coopera-tive, the process of minimizing nuclear dangers will be stopped after the START follow-on treaty and the NPT review conference in May 2010. All the talk of a world without nuclear weapons will become an ironic joke. This bears repeating. If the US, Russia and China cannot establish strategic cooperation, the salience and number of nuclear weapons will not decrease and the non-proliferation regime will weaken.[18]

Russia and the West

US–Russian cooperation is the key to building a broader global partnership to achieve progressive denuclearisation. The United States and Russia together possess more than 90% of the nuclear weapons in the world. More importantly, their cooperation and partnership in working with other states to promote and implement a policy of progressive denuclearisation is indispensable to achieving global consensus and multilateral implementation. Realising these ambitions will depend on whether the US and Russia can succeed in reviving political cooperation and the strategic arms reduction process.

Trust and cooperation between Moscow and Washington have declined. After a brief honeymoon at the end of the Cold War, East–West political relations reverted to a pattern of tension and policy disagreement. Many factors contributed to this change, including the expansive foreign policy of the US, the enlargement of NATO, the return to more authoritarian rule within Russia, Moscow's attempts to exert control over its 'near abroad', policy differences over Kosovo and the North Caucasus, and disputes over the tactical nuclear weapons and conventional forces in Europe. US–Russian relations were particularly icy during the George W. Bush administration, but they have improved slightly with the Obama administration's 'reset' policy and greater recognition in Washington that non-proliferation and disarmament objectives will not be met without Russia's cooperation.

As the United States and Russia attempt to build trust, they can rely on a proven historical model: negotiated arms control. As Perkovich observes, these mechanisms have been tried and tested and can be made to work again.[19] The Obama administration has followed that advice with its emphasis on the negotiation of a new START. The force reductions in the treaty are modest, but the agreement preserves vital verification and monitoring protocols that are crucial to future arms limitation. The bargaining process provided a venue in which the two sides could discuss their differences and avoid the misunderstandings and unjustified fears that can result from a lack of dialogue. Stanford University researcher Pavel Podwig has argued that the verification and transparency mechanisms in the treaty are more important than any specific number of mandated warheads.[20] The new treaty could set a pattern for future agreements, which the White House has pledged to pursue, to reduce reliance on nuclear weapons and enhance strategic cooperation.

Improved US–Russian cooperation will require solutions to fundamental disagreements over the role of nuclear weapons in European security. During the Cold War the United States and NATO deployed thousands of tactical nuclear weapons in Europe as a deterrent against the overwhelming conventional military threat posed by vast Soviet conventional forces, which were considered superior to those of the West. In the post-Cold War era the tables have turned. Russian conventional strength has declined in recent decades relative to the expanding ranks of NATO. Political leaders in Moscow have adopted a view similar to that of NATO in earlier decades. Nuclear weapons have consequently assumed increased importance as a deterrent against NATO's overwhelming conventional advantage.

Russia still deploys approximately 2,000 tactical nuclear weapons, many of them positioned for potential use in the European theatre. NATO maintains a smaller force of between 150 and 240 tactical nuclear weapons.[21] Proposals have been offered for the elimination of these weapons, but NATO ministers have opposed the suggestions as contrary to the doctrine of flexible response and extended deterrence. Central European members of NATO in particular have argued for the maintenance of the US nuclear umbrella as a vital defence against possible Russian aggression or intimidation. There is practically no opposition to the nuclear dimension of NATO, but there is disagreement on what it means.

Germany recently stated its support for the withdrawal of tactical nuclear weapons from its territory, as part of the programme of the new government elected in October 2009. Previous governments had only gone as far as to raise questions about continued US nuclear deployments. Berlin placed the recent initiative within the context of growing international support for nuclear disarmament and specifically referred to Obama's proposals for the goal of a world without nuclear weapons. A government spokesman described the policy as a disarmament measure and a contribution to the fulfillment of commitments under the NPT.[22]

NATO could in principle easily end its reliance on nuclear deterrence, given the Alliance's overwhelming conventional military superiority. The United States and its allies have more than sufficient conventional military strength to respond to potential security threats from Russia or other states. Conventional forces would be able to meet military threats with more targeted and calibrated power than nuclear arms. As Müller observes: 'NATO could move to no first use and the withdrawal of tactical nuclear weapons from territories of their nonnuclear allies without any loss in alliance security. With that, the time-honoured option to use nuclear weapons first could fall by the wayside.'[23] Turkey and the states on Russia's periphery would be nervous about such a change. They still see deterrent value in NATO's small force of tactical nuclear weapons on European soil. These states deserve and need security assurances, but these can be provided more reliably by non-nuclear means.

In the 1990s, Russia and NATO began to establish a rudimentary architecture of security cooperation. In 1994 Russia joined the Partnership for Peace programme as a step towards defence cooperation with NATO. In 1995 Russia agreed to participate in the NATO-led Implementation Force (IFOR) in Bosnia. In 1997 Russian President Boris Yeltsin joined with 16 NATO leaders to sign the NATO–Russia Founding Act, which promised greater cooperation on a range of security policies. That year also saw creation of the Euro-Atlantic Partnership Council, which in 2002 became the NATO–Russia Council. These efforts helped to establish venues for dialogue and communication but they could not transcend underlying policy differences. In the decade following the 1999 Kosovo crisis political tensions have increased and cooperation has become more tenuous. The 2008 crisis in Georgia led to the discontinuation of the council's work, which was gradually restarted in March 2009. In the Russian view, the NATO–Russia Council needs more 'value-added' and should play a greater role in addressing East–West strategic issues.

One of the keys to building more cooperative relations with Russia may be the simple act of providing negative security assurances against conventional or nuclear attack, provided Moscow does not threaten or attack NATO member states. Numerous specific policy steps could be pursued to advance security cooperation. The same assurances are needed from Russia towards NATO. These include:

- negotiating additional nuclear arms reduction agreements, dismantling weapons on reserve and eliminating classes of weapons such as short-range tactical arms;
- developing plans for a grand bargain on missile defences in which the United States agrees to suspend additional deployments, pending agreement and implementation of deep reductions down to near-zero levels, with the two sides developing modalities and mechanisms for shared defences; and

- pursuing negotiations to restructure the Treaty on Conventional Armed Forces in Europe and developing additional confidence-building measures.

Reassuring China

China has proclaimed a policy of so-called 'peaceful rise' and asserts that its growing power does not threaten any nation. China's record on nuclear-weapons policy is mixed, however. On the one hand, China has adopted a restrained policy towards its nuclear capabilities, consistently maintaining a relatively small arsenal estimated to be in the range of 250 warheads. On the other hand, Beijing has steadily modernised and upgraded its conventional military and nuclear-weapons capabilities. In the past China provided support for nuclear proliferation, aiding the development of Pakistan's missile and nuclear-weapons programmes. In recent years Beijing has improved its non-proliferation record and has been admitted to the Nuclear Suppliers Group. Chinese government leaders provide reassurances to other leaders of their peaceful intensions, but military officials have at times issued bellicose statements and engaged in provocative acts.[24]

China has cooperated in some non-proliferation efforts, helping to host the Six-Party Talks on North Korea, but generally it has adopted an independent line. In the UN Conference on Disarmament it has insisted on linking discussion of a Fissile Material Cut-off Treaty to negotiations for a treaty banning the deployment of weapons in outer space. It has supported sanctions against Iran on some occasions, but not on others. Chinese officials and experts reflect an ambivalent attitude towards non-proliferation and disarmament. The country has traditionally supported the goal of disarmament, and recently endorsed Obama's call for a world without nuclear weapons. Preventing the spread of nuclear weapons is in Beijing's interest because it helps to preserve its superiority over potential regional rivals. It also advances its goal of a more 'harmonious world', and provides leverage with the United States and Europe. Yet Chinese officials are highly critical of the inequalities in the NPT regime and global power relations generally. Some see the spread of nuclear weapons as inevitable and a way to balance the hegemony and growing military and nuclear superiority of the United States.[25]

Bates Gill, an expert on Chinese foreign policy, has argued that the United States should adopt a more conciliatory and cooperative policy towards China, acknowledging its rise to global power as an unavoidable fact and seeking to engage it as a global partner rather than strategic rival.[26] Some in Washington see China as a global competitor, the principal rival to US primacy and a power to be contained. The 2002 National Security Strategy of the United States calls for 'dissuading future military competition' to prevent the rise of global rivals.[27] Accompanying this doctrine is Washington's global-strike capacity, which gives the United States unprecedented means to launch remote-control strikes anywhere in the world with conventional or nuclear weapons. This strategic capacity and the US reluctance to ban weapons in space are not only deeply worrying to China, they impede security cooperation.

To gain greater Chinese cooperation for non-proliferation and disarmament, the United States will need to provide security assurances, making clear that it has no intention of challenging or attacking China militarily so long as it does not threaten US security or that of US allies. A range of confidence-building and security-reassurance measures are available to improve US–Chinese relations and increase the likelihood of cooperation in nuclear non-proliferation and disarmament. These include:
- Bilateral discussions on nuclear doctrine, space cooperation and missile defences;

- Renewed military-to-military contacts and exchanges and joint military exercises and observations;
- Renewed lab-to-lab discussions on nuclear management and verification mechanisms for implementation of test-ban and fissile-material agreements. [28]

Conclusion

The discourse of nuclear policy often has an unreal character. For many the idea of preserving peace through the threat of mass annihilation is difficult to accept, logically and morally. The ambiguities of nuclear discourse are particularly sharp in the differing understandings of how to assure security. In official nuclear doctrine, security depends on the maintenance of nuclear deterrence, with its vow to use nuclear weapons if necessary to deter attack and defend allies. Without nuclear security assurances, it is assumed, states will be vulnerable to intimidation or attack and allies will seek alternative alliance partners or attempt to acquire their own weapons. Sceptics counter that the very existence of nuclear weapons threatens security, and that alternative means are available for deterring attack and protecting allies without reliance on nuclear weapons.

The orthodoxy of security-through-nuclear-deterrence may have had meaning in an earlier era, when Winston Churchill famously declared in his final speech as Prime Minister on defence that 'safety will be the sturdy child of terror, and survival the twin brother of annihilation'.[29] In a multipolar age of proliferation dangers and terrorism, however, this strategy has become increasingly irrelevant and counterproductive. The NPT was built on the basis of assurances from the NWS not to use nuclear weapons against NNWS. The treaty's permanent extension was made possible by the reiteration of those assurances. The continued viability of the non-proliferation regime and of global security in general depends upon maintaining and strengthening assurances against nuclear weapons use. This will depend upon building international cooperation and developing non-nuclear means of deterring threats and protecting allies.

CHAPTER SIX

Addressing Regional Challenges

The goal of achieving a world without nuclear weapons is strongly challenged by the actions of the three states that are outside the NPT (Israel, India and Pakistan), by the withdrawal from the treaty of North Korea and by the risks posed by Iran's developing nuclear programme. These challenges can be grouped into three regional settings – South Asia, Northeast Asia and the Middle East – and need to be addressed in the context of political and security conditions within those regions. Ultimately, each regional challenge will need to be solved to reach the goal of nuclear zero, but it is not necessary to defer or postpone progress on global disarmament until the regional challenges are fully resolved. Both processes, regional and global, can proceed simultaneously. Progress in one arena will likely encourage progress in the other. The enhanced global cooperation that is needed to move towards general disarmament will help to reduce tensions in the regional settings, and vice versa. Improved security cooperation in the Middle East and in South and East Asia will make it easier for the nuclear-weapons states to feel secure in reducing and ending their reliance on nuclear deterrence.

Nuclear arming in South Asia

The nuclear arms race in South Asia is an enormous challenge to the prospects for global disarmament. Contrary to the trend between the United States and Russia, India and Pakistan are expanding their arsenals and developing ever more elaborate launch capabilities. India has begun sea trials of its 6,000-metric-ton nuclear-powered submarine, the *Arihant* (*Destroyer of Enemies*), the first of several planned missile-firing submarines.[1] It is expanding its military spending and now has the world's tenth-largest military budget. Pakistan is desperately attempting to keep pace and has developed a nuclear arsenal estimated at between 70 and 90 weapons.[2] Both countries remain locked in a bitter strategic rivalry that has produced two major wars, numerous skirmishes and a continuing Indian military occupation and Pakistani-supported insurgency in Kashmir. The nuclear competition in the region also involves China, which India sees as a strategic rival. India seeks to gain strategic parity with its northern neighbour, while Pakistan's nuclear programme is entirely oriented towards keeping pace with India.

US non-proliferation policies in the region over the course of three decades have been erratic, inconsistent and ultimately ineffective. Washington attempted to combine denial strategies – blocking exports to India and Pakistan of sensitive equipment and materials – and various economic and security assistance programmes. Technology controls and sanctions made nuclear development more difficult and costly and perhaps slowed it down, but could not stop it. Conflicting agendas were a constant problem of US policy. Non-proliferation goals often clashed with other economic or strategic interests in the subcontinent. The commitment to sanctions flagged when their political costs appeared too high.

In the 1980s, when Pakistan's help was needed to aid mujahadeen rebels fighting Soviet forces in Afghanistan, non-proliferation restrictions were tossed aside. The floodgates swung open and lavish US assistance poured in ($5.4 billion in mostly military aid from 1982 to 1990),[3] passing through the hands of senior Pakistani military and intelligence officials who in some cases were supporters of the nuclear programme and of A.Q. Khan, leader of a global smuggling network accused of selling nuclear technology. The huge US aid programme was a counterproductive incentive, rewarding the centres of power in Pakistan least sympathetic to Western non-proliferation interests and to the broader goal of promoting democracy, human rights and equitable development. The same pattern emerged in the aftermath of the terrorist attacks of 9/11. The United States depended heavily on Pakistan's military government as a principal ally in overthrowing the Taliban regime in Afghanistan, and continues to rely on its help in the fight against the Taliban and al-Qaeda. This has made Washington reluctant to challenge Islamabad's nuclear policies, or to press for more accountability and transparency in shutting down the Khan network.

US non-proliferation law required the imposition of sanctions when India and Pakistan tested nuclear weapons in 1998. This effort was half-hearted and short-lived. It conflicted with other US policies in the region, including growing commercial engagement with India and continued strategic partnership with Pakistan. Soon after the sanctions were imposed in May and June 1998 – banning loans, military assistance, investment and technology transfers – Congress granted an exemption for grain-export credits and guarantees. President Bill Clinton followed by suspending sanctions altogether in July 1998. The many interests in the United States favouring engagement in South Asia made any substantial US sanctions effort extremely difficult. A similar dynamic exists in other countries where broader interests in strategic engagement outweigh a narrow focus on counter-proliferation sanctions.

A flawed deal

The Indo-US nuclear agreement, signed in 2005, confers de facto recognition on India as a nuclear-weapons state. Washington's principal motivation was geostrategic: to strengthen the bilateral relationship as a bulwark against a rising China. The deal also offered commercial opportunities to sell nuclear technology and expertise to the market of a major growing economy. To make this deal acceptable New Delhi has agreed to place its civilian nuclear facilities under IAEA safeguards, but it has not accepted monitoring of its extensive nuclear weapon-related facilities. The deal makes India the only country ever to receive officially sanctioned nuclear assistance despite having developed nuclear weapons and refusing to sign the NPT.

The provision of nuclear assistance to India under these conditions was a violation of US non-proliferation laws, which had to be changed to accommodate the deal. It also violated rules of the Nuclear Suppliers Group (NSG) that require full-scope safeguards as a condition of supply; a waiver was granted in a contentious NSG decision in 2008. The US–India agreement is contrary to the spirit of Article IV of the NPT, which envisions assistance for nuclear energy as compensation for the disavowal of nuclear weapons. Offering such assistance to a state openly defying the standards nearly every other state has accepted weakens the international non-proliferation norm. It also sets a potentially dangerous precedent of major states providing nuclear assistance to strategic allies without regard for non-proliferation standards.

The nuclear deal is an established fact and cannot be reversed, so the challenge now is to use it to advance the overall goal of denuclearisation. As Harald Müller notes, the deal could open the door to closer collaboration with India to achieve the goal all previous Indian leaders have espoused, a universal and equitable global disarmament and non-proliferation regime. India should be offered a seat at the table and encouraged to serve as a co-leader in global efforts to end reliance on nuclear weapons.[4]

Persuading Pyongyang

Throughout the frustrating years of attempts to restrain North Korea's nuclear programme, Pyongyang has displayed a consistent pattern of threat-based diplomacy. As Leon Sigal has observed, 'North Korea often floats concessions on a tide of threats'.[5] Isolated and vulnerable in a post-Cold War world, feeling threatened by continued US enmity and military deployments in the region, political leaders in Pyongyang have sought to achieve security and preserve their power by threatening Washington and then offering to bargain away their weapons in exchange for a lifeline of diplomatic and economic survival.

On numerous occasions over the years North Korean officials have stated explicitly their willingness to abandon weapons programmes in return for US security assurances and guarantees of a more normalised relationship. In June 1998, after testing a long-range ballistic missile, a North Korean statement declared, 'if the United States really wants to prevent our missile exports, it should lift the economic embargo as early as possible, and make a compensation for the losses to be caused by discontinued missile exports'.[6] In August 2003 during Six Party negotiations, North Korean negotiator Kim Yong Il declared, 'we can dismantle our nuclear programme if the United States makes a switchover in its hostile policy towards us and does not pose any threat to us'.[7]

Relations between Pyongyang and Washington often follow a tit-for-tat pattern: conciliatory action bringing improvement;

confrontation breeding hostility. When Washington offered concessions, as in the 1994 Agreed Framework or the 2005 Statement of Principles, Pyongyang responded by partially restraining its weapons programme. When Washington reneged on its commitments or made threats, such as President George W. Bush's inclusion of North Korea on a list of states that sponsor terrorism in 2002, Pyongyang responded by rejecting non-proliferation constraints and accelerating the development of its weapons programmes.

The Agreed Framework of October 1994 was successful for a time in shutting down the North Korean nuclear programme. Under the terms of the agreement, the United States and its partners offered to provide North Korea with shipments of fuel oil and agreed to construct two new, less proliferation-prone nuclear reactors. The United States also pledged to 'move towards full normalization of political and economic relations', that is, to begin lifting economic sanctions and opening the doors to trade and diplomatic recognition. In exchange, Pyongyang agreed to halt nuclear production activities and the reprocessing of spent fuel rods. It pledged to shut down its graphite-moderated nuclear reactors, and withdrew its threat to pull out of the NPT. It accepted full-scope safeguards that consisted of IAEA monitoring and inspection of designated nuclear facilities.[8]

The agreement soon began to unravel, however. The North complied with its pledges to halt plutonium production and permitted international monitoring of the freeze,[9] but it violated the pledge to shut down its nuclear programme by pursuing a secret uranium-enrichment programme. US implementation of the agreement lagged, in part because of a political backlash against being seen to appease the North after Republicans gained control of Congress in midterm elections in 1994. Washington fell behind on promised deliveries of fuel oil and was unable to improve diplomatic ties, in part because of constant stumbling blocks and acts of defiance from the North.

During a visit to the region, then Defense Secretary William Perry concluded that 'the way to achieve these aims is to reassure North Korea and satisfy its security and economic concerns'.[10] In its final years in office the Clinton administration began to take steps towards the easing of some economic sanctions, and Madeleine Albright became the first US Secretary of State to visit North Korea. The administration was unable to reach agreement before leaving office, however, largely due to the difficulties of negotiating with the Pyongyang regime and the legacy of mistrust between the two sides. Pyongyang's obstructionism has been systematic, encompassing major and minor issues, which has made it difficult for outside powers to establish a predictable and forward-looking relationship with the North.

The Bush administration initially rejected the strategy of incentives-based diplomacy. In 2002 Bush declared North Korea part of the 'axis of evil'. Washington halted the delivery of fuel oil in response to Pyongyang's uranium-enrichment programme, which violated the Agreed Framework. The North then withdrew from the NPT, expelled international inspectors, resumed the reprocessing of spent fuel and accelerated its efforts to develop nuclear weapons and ballistic missiles. The Bush administration was initially wary of bilateral talks with the North and developed instead the Six-Party Talks as a useful framework for regional non-proliferation diplomacy.

In September 2005 the parties to the talks signed a 'Statement of Principles'. This included a pledge from the North to abandon its nuclear programme and return to the NPT, and a security-assurance declaration from the United States that it had no intention of attacking the North with nuclear or conventional weapons. This negative security assurance was a significant gesture from the United States. The two sides differed over details of the plan, however, and were unable to agree on a new settlement. The North proceeded to conduct its first nuclear test in 2006 (another followed in 2009) and also tested long-range ballistic missiles.

A further twist in the plot came in February 2007, when agreement was reached on initial actions to implement the Statement of Principles. The agreement included the familiar pattern of reciprocal obligations. The North pledged to abandon its nuclear programme, in exchange for a package of incentives that included the provision of energy assistance. It began to disable some of its nuclear facilities and staged for the media an explosion at the Yongbyon nuclear site that destroyed a 20-metre cooling tower. The United States lifted some sanctions and removed North Korea from the list of states sponsoring terrorism, but implementation of these actions was interrupted by the Presidential nomination campaign in the US and the winding-down of the Bush administration, and therefore the impasse remained.

A definitive solution to the North Korea proliferation crisis will be difficult to achieve short of a fundamental change in the nature of the regime. According to Victor Cha, former deputy US negotiator during the Six-Party Talks, Pyongyang has been unwilling to accept past incentives and security assurances from Washington because it wants something more fundamental – political survival. It wants the United States to help prop up its corrupt and faltering regime. Pyongyang needs to open up to the West to survive, but it is unwilling to do so for fear that this will only hasten its own demise. Its major bargaining chip is the nuclear programme, but negotiating it away will leave it powerless. Definitive denuclearisation is thus unlikely in the near future, but this does not mean that diplomatic options should be abandoned. The primary focus, Cha argues, should be 'freezing, disabling and degrading' the North's nuclear programme.[11] For this purpose the rigorous international sanctions adopted under UN Security Council Resolution 1874 (2009) are useful. They limit the North's access to weapons technology and impede its ability to earn revenues from international weapons trafficking.

These and other containment approaches might be combined with a diplomatic bargaining process designed to induce more lasting concessions from the North. The United States could take the lead in developing a GRIT strategy (graduated reciprocation in tension reduction) by renewing security assurances and promises of normalised diplomatic and commercial relations. Taking the initiative would put Washington more in control of the diplomatic process and render it less vulnerable to the vagaries of Pyongyang's erratic threat-based behaviour. The United States could take action to suspend some of its sanctions on the North or postpone military exercises in the region, and wait for the other side to respond. If the North acted provocatively or attempted to take advantage of the gesture, the United States could withdraw the action and return to the status quo ante. If the North responded positively, the United States could take additional steps and attempt to induce further concessions. The goal would be to establish a pattern of reciprocal concessions that would aim towards the negotiation of a comprehensive agreement for the dismantlement of North Korea's weapons programmes, the reduction of military tensions in the region and the normalisation of diplomatic and economic relations. The result of such a process would be a significant enhancement of security in the region and a dramatic step towards strengthening the international non-proliferation regime.

Iran: diffusing the dispute

The confrontation over Iran's nuclear programme is arguably the most dangerous in the world. If Iran were to get the bomb, Arab states in the region would likely follow suit and Israel would be tempted to launch military strikes, as would some policymakers in Washington. The consequences of such events would be catastrophic for the region and the world. Resolving the Iranian dispute, on the other hand, could be of decisive importance to regional and global non-proliferation efforts. If Iran and the major powers could end the stand-off, political and military tensions in the region would subside, the global non-proliferation regime would get a boost and the path to global disarmament would widen.

A solution to the conflict is not likely in the near future, given the unstable and divisive political situation within Iran. Yet the core ingredients of a future solution can be envisioned: assurances from Iran, rigorously verified, that its nuclear programme is entirely peaceful; a willingness by the United States and the European Union to accommodate Iran's desire for uranium enrichment; and an end to the decades-long enmity between Iran and the United States, leading to normalised diplomatic and commercial relations. These steps will be difficult to accept for political leaders on both sides, but the potential benefits are significant.

The consideration of alternative strategies begins with a more sober assessment of the nuclear threat. Iran is developing a large-scale nuclear industry and has failed to comply fully with its obligations to the IAEA. Questions about possible military connections to its nuclear programme remain unanswered. Yet there is no confirmation that Tehran is actually building nuclear weapons. US intelligence agencies concluded in their official National Intelligence Estimate (NIE) for 2007 that Iran halted its alleged nuclear-weapons programme in 2003. This assessment was confirmed in March 2009 during testimony by Admiral Dennis Blair, Director of National Intelligence, before the Senate Armed Services Committee. In 2010, however, there were indications that the US intelligence community would revise this assessment with a new NIE concluding that Iran may be resuming research on weaponisation.[12] Until February 2010, Iran had enriched uranium only to the level required for nuclear power production, less than 5% uranium-235. By re-enriching this low-level fuel to highly enriched uranium (90% U-235), it would be able to produce nuclear weapons. In February 2010, Tehran began efforts to enrich to 20%, on the grounds that this was needed for replacement fuel for the Tehran Research Reactor. Iran's de facto rejection of an agreement in principle reached in October 2009 to exchange the bulk of its low-enriched uranium stockpile for research reactor fuel via Russia and France was a worrisome indication of the regime's latent capability to produce fissile material for nuclear weapons and raised further questions about its intentions.

Although Iran has refused to disclose information demanded by the IAEA about past activities, it has allowed the inspections minimally required by its safeguards agreement and at times has accepted more rigorous inspections. In 2003 Iran consented to the Additional Protocol, but it suspended its participation in 2006 when the IAEA reported Iran's safeguards violations to the Security Council. In 2007 Iran increased its cooperation with agency inspectors as a part of a special 'work programme' to clarify questions about its past nuclear activities. In November 2007, then IAEA Director General Mohamed ElBaradei reported 'good progress' in examining these past activities, although he also expressed concern about a lack of full disclosure on crucial issues related to potential weaponisation.[13] In August 2009 Iran accepted long-standing IAEA requests for access to the heavy-water nuclear reactor under construction at Arak and for greater access to its commercial-scale uranium-enrichment plant at Natanz.

These gestures of partial cooperation are signs that, despite acts of defiance and obstruction, Iran is willing selectively to cooperate with the IAEA and the international community. Most of what is known about the Iranian nuclear programme has come from IAEA monitoring on the ground. ElBaradei expressed confidence in the ability of inspectors to monitor Iran's declared enrichment activities at Natanz. This is an important assurance of international ability to detect declared enrichment activities.[14] Keeping Iran within the NPT inspection regime and persuading the country to return to the Additional Protocol are high priorities for international diplomacy. This is essential for addressing widespread suspicions that Iran may be involved in prohibited nuclear weapons-related activities.

Iran and the United States, with its European allies, are playing a cat-and-mouse game in which Tehran is revealing only those facilities that have been discovered by Western intelligence or other international actors. This creates constant uncertainty and speculation regarding the true intentions of Iran, which seems deliberately to build its policy on unexpected moves. Due to its character as an international agency, the IAEA seems ready to accept some Iranian reassurances, but at the same time it has pursued other avenues to gain a better grip on what Tehran is really up to. This combination of avoidance and reassurance means that it is difficult to reach any firm agreement with Iran within the NPT framework.

Since 2009, new concerns have surfaced about Iran's inadequate compliance with IAEA safeguards. In September 2009 Iran belatedly announced construction of an additional pilot enrichment plant near Qom. It did so only after unmistakable evidence of the plant's existence became known to Western intelligence agencies. The government said it had decided to build the underground enrichment site because threats of military attacks had been made against Iran. Tehran provided IAEA inspectors full access to the site, which enabled the agency to verify its design, but the agency's Board of Governors rebuked Iran for not disclosing the site earlier and demanded a halt to construction.[15] The IAEA determined that Tehran's failure to inform the agency of the additional site when design and construction first began several years earlier was 'inconsistent with its obligations' under previously signed agreements. The agency's latest reports continue to express concern that Iran has not provided requested information that would enable the agency to exclude the possibility of military dimensions to Iran's nuclear programme.[16]

Iranian policy may appear irrationally truculent to officials in the West, but the view from Tehran is very different. The country has faced hostility from the United States for 30 years and sees large-scale US military forces deployed on its eastern and western borders and in the Persian Gulf and nearby seas. In 2007 the White House reportedly authorised covert CIA operations to destabilise the Iranian government.[17] Seymour Hersh reported in July 2008 that the US Congress funded a $400 million major escalation of covert operations against Iran.[18] The existence of external threats makes it difficult for Iranian officials to compromise and for opposition activists to speak out against the nuclear programme. Those who might favour accommodation with the West can be accused of disloyalty.

To date US diplomacy towards Iran has relied primarily on sanctions and the threat of military force. The UN Security Council has imposed several waves of targeted sanctions against designated Iranian officials and agencies. The incentives provided by the European Union and the United States had by April 2010 failed to alter Iranian policy. Lessons from other non-proliferation cases suggest that incentives-based diplomacy is more likely to be effective in achieving denuclearisation than an emphasis on sanctions and coercive measures, but the Iran stand-off so far defies comparison with other models.

The instability and deep divisions that have emerged within Iranian society following the disputed 2009 presidential election compound these problems and complicate attempts to influence Tehran's nuclear policy. Lessons from other non-proliferation cases indicate that denuclearisation is more likely to occur when governing regimes are more democratic and oriented towards free-market engagement with the West. Iranian society is deeply divided over these questions. Some factions favour accommodation and integration with the international community, but they have been marginalised politically.

Leading political opponents of the current regime in Tehran have opposed further sanctions as counterproductive. In a September 2009 statement, defeated presidential candidate Mir Hossein Mousavi said: 'These sanctions would not be against a government but the people who have already been agonized by this government'.[19] Moussavi and fellow opposition leader Mehdi Karroubi have declared their support for Iranian development of nuclear technology, including the right to enrichment, although they have been critical of the Tehran regime's provocative policies and have called for transparency and compliance with IAEA standards.

Achieving a diplomatic solution to the current nuclear stand-off may require acceptance of limited uranium enrichment. The P3 (the US, UK and France) and Germany have demanded that Tehran end its enrichment programme, but Iran already has an enrichment capacity. Under Article IV of the NPT Iran is legally entitled to develop a nuclear industry, provided it is in compliance with its safeguards obligations. Iranian officials across the political spectrum support enrichment as an 'inalienable right'.

Insistence on an absolute ban on enrichment has become an obstacle to potential agreement.

George Perkovich and Pierre Goldschmidt suggested in October 2009 that the Security Council may wish to amend its resolutions to 'allow Iran to continue its ongoing practice of enriching uranium to less than 5%', provided Tehran agrees to the most rigorous verification standards.[20] The proposed amendment would be linked to renewed Iranian acceptance of the Additional Protocol, which would provide further confidence in the IAEA's ability to detect clandestine enrichment. The value of this suggestion has been undermined by the Iranian government's efforts to begin enriching uranium to the level of 20%.

The challenges of improving political relations with Iran are formidable. The essential goal is to gain greater Iranian compliance with IAEA standards and Security Council resolutions. Recent political developments in Tehran, however, indicate that the present regime has little intention of cooperating effectively with external powers and international bodies. Tehran is cracking down on its internal opposition and attempting to parry external pressures. An expectation seems to prevail in Tehran that China and perhaps Russia can be counted on to oppose further Security Council sanctions. Current trends within Iran may not be sustainable, however, and international actors should have diplomatic cards ready to play if new political opportunities appear in Iran.

In such a situation, Washington might consider easing some of the many unilateral sanctions it has in place. It could end hostile operations that may be under way and stop penalising Iranian banks. Any conciliatory gestures from Washington should be conditioned on reciprocation from Tehran. If Iran were to respond positively to US actions, further initiatives could be taken. Otherwise the status quo would be maintained, with the continuation of UN Security Council sanctions. The problem is that sanctions-based policies in the past have not been effective. US unilateral measures have not altered the regime's policies, and UN measures so far have had little impact. Incentive offers have also failed so far, but perhaps more substantive offers might have greater impact. The acceptance of low-level enrichment, conditioned on greater Iranian transparency, would coincide with the position of Moussavi and other reform leaders within Iran and perhaps provide a form of international encouragement to the opposition. The options and prospects for non-proliferation success are limited, but the urgency of finding a solution requires further, more intensive diplomatic efforts.

Middle East peace

The goal of preventing nuclear-weapons development in Iran is linked to broader denuclearisation efforts in the region and globally. Political dynamics in the Middle East are extremely complex, rooted in the most intractable disputes and risks of further nuclear proliferation and armed conflict. Profound dissatisfaction exists among Arab states over Israel's unequal status as the only nuclear-armed state in the region. Israel's nuclear defence capability, comprising an arsenal of approximately 100 nuclear weapons and sophisticated weapons delivery systems, is a constant source of perceived danger. This compounds the pervasive sense of humiliation and frustration that has existed for many years among Arab governments and populations in the region. For Israelis the hostility of Arabs has created a siege mentality and a determination to defend the nation by any and all means.

For decades Arab political leaders have argued for a nuclear weapons-free zone in the Middle East, and they continue to make this demand in the context of the Non-proliferation

Treaty review conferences. Israel and the United States have argued that disarmament in the region must be preceded by a comprehensive peace agreement in which Arab states agree to accept and live peacefully with the state of Israel. In February 1995, just prior to the indefinite extension of the NPT, then Foreign Minister Shimon Peres declared that Israel would be willing to start negotiating the establishment of a Middle East Nuclear Weapons-Free Zone 'two years' after the signing of a comprehensive peace agreement in the region.[21]

Israel developed its nuclear weapons, and clings to them today, out of the perception of an existential threat to its survival. As Avner Cohen writes, 'Israel's nuclear project was conceived in the shadow of the Holocaust, and the lessons of the Holocaust provided the justification and motivation for the project'.[22] One of the architects of the Israeli state and its first prime minister, David Ben-Gurion, was driven by these concerns. The military threat from the Arab states has eased in recent decades, but other threats have emerged from Iran and from the rise of Hizbullah in Southern Lebanon and Hamas in Gaza. Israeli concerns for security are legitimate, and its reluctance to lay down its nuclear arms without a lasting regional peace is understandable, but, as Müller writes, 'it is much harder to sympathise with occupation policies which stand in the way of any move towards such an endurable peaceful relationship'.[23]

No progress on a nuclear weapons-free zone in the Middle East will be possible without a broader peace settlement in the region. That will not happen without active leadership from the United States, which may be the only country capable of persuading Israel to change its policies and convincing the Palestinian Authority and neighbouring Arab states to accept Israeli compromises – although even Washington's influence is limited in this regard. The Obama administration has exerted some pressure on Israel to end illegal settlements in the West Bank and Jerusalem, but much more vigorous efforts will be needed. When and if the bitter differences over settlements are resolved, the parties can begin to negotiate a comprehensive peace deal, with active support and encouragement from the United Nations, the United States, the European Union and other external parties. An agreement structured along the lines of the Arab initiative first proposed by Saudi Arabia in 2002 would be a sine qua non for any consideration of a nuclear weapons-free zone in the region.

Conclusion

Regional challenges confirm the relevance of non-proliferation to global security. In each of the regions examined, the dispute over nuclear-weapons development has been and remains a source of acute anxiety and instability. In the cases of Iran and North Korea, a crisis over nuclear proliferation could lead to armed hostilities and a dramatic worsening of regional and global security. In Pakistan the nightmare scenario is partial state collapse leading to terrorist acquisition of nuclear weapons. If instability in Pakistan became endemic, it would be difficult to predict and contain India's reaction, which could be military in nature. Many dark visions are conceivable in these cases, all of them pointing to the urgency of more concerted efforts to resolve these disputes and prevent any further spread of the bomb.

Attempts to address regional proliferation challenges are at the top of the international policy agenda at the United Nations, in the European Union, in the United States and in many other countries. Despite all this effort little progress has been achieved in resolving the issues and encouraging nuclear rollback. To the contrary, India and Pakistan continue to enlarge their arsenals, North Korea remains defiant, and Iran is steadily expanding its nuclear-production capability. To date multilateral diplomatic attempts to pressure and persuade North Korea and Iran have not worked. This does not mean that unilateral military measures would be any more effective.

No magical formula is available to resolve these challenges, but the most important common factor in each is the role of the United States and its ability to persuade other major powers to join the international quest for nuclear dismantlement. Especially in the cases of North Korea and Iran, a change in US policy could be decisive in altering proliferation dynamics. In each case the solution may lie in a shift from reliance on coercive pressures towards greater consideration of positive inducements. The analysis of these cases and the record of other examples of nuclear reversal suggest that security assurances could be particularly important. Lessons from other cases also confirm the importance of conciliatory initiatives in generating patterns of positive reciprocity. Steps towards the normalisation of diplomatic relations, a scaling back of military threats and deployments, the suspension of certain sanctions measures – such steps could help to defuse the crises and encourage political settlements.

Of course any significant concessions to North Korea or Iran will be sharply criticised as appeasement. South Korea and Israel will insist that their security concerns are addressed. The proposed inducements would not be strategic concessions but small steps towards tension reduction, which could be reversed if the recipient country attempts to take advantage. As Hans Morgenthau observed, the practice of offering concessions can be a useful tool of diplomacy so long as it does not confer advantages to an aggressor or imperialist power.[24] When the most powerful state offers inducements to the weak, this is not appeasement but wise diplomacy and a potential means of seeking breakthroughs for non-proliferation and disarmament.

CHAPTER SEVEN

Building Cooperation for Non-proliferation and Disarmament

It is easy to be discouraged or cynical about the call for a world without nuclear weapons. The goal seems so utopian, the obstacles so formidable, the risks so great that some are inclined to dismiss the whole enterprise as politically and technically impossible. Yet many of the steps that are needed to realise the goal of disarmament are directly relevant to current non-proliferation challenges. The policies that are being implemented now to strengthen the NPT and prevent the spread of nuclear weapons are the same measures that can guide the world towards diminished reliance on nuclear weapons, and to their eventual elimination. In this chapter we review some of these near-term policies and consider ways to enhance their effectiveness. Stronger international verification systems, multinational nuclear-fuel guarantees, robust cooperative-threat reduction programmes, universal ratification of the nuclear test ban – all are achievable objectives that can improve global security in the near term and pave the way towards disarmament over the long term.

The role of the IAEA

The IAEA is a vital global agency for monitoring compliance with non-proliferation safeguards. The agency has scored

important successes in identifying nuclear cheating and helping
to implement disarmament and non-proliferation goals. In Iraq
in the 1990s the IAEA identified and dismantled Iraq's nuclear-
weapons facilities; in 2002 when inspections resumed the
agency verified that Iraq had no nuclear weapons or production
facilities. In North Korea the agency discovered violations of
IAEA safeguards agreements and the development of reprocessing capabilities beyond those admitted by the Pyongyang
regime. In recent years the agency traced uranium isotopes on
equipment in Libya to the nuclear smuggling syndicate of A.Q.
Khan. The IAEA has exposed questionable nuclear activities
in Iran and pressured the regime to comply fully with inspections protocols and negotiated agreements. In these and other
tasks the agency has been indispensable in monitoring global
compliance with non-proliferation agreements.

The IAEA's authority and capacity are limited, however.
The agency's safeguards provisions concerning the inspection
of nuclear facilities are weak. They require the consent of the
target state and only apply to 'declared' facilities which the
state identifies. According to the report of the independent
commission on the role of the IAEA, the agency's safeguards
are 'not designed to ensure either safety or guarding'. Nor does
it have the capability to prevent nuclear materials from being
stolen. 'No programme exists in which safeguards inspectors systematically report any security weaknesses they may
observe.' Agreements with states provide that, in return for
the authorisation to conduct inspections, the agency will use
the information only for safeguards purposes and will keep it
confidential.[1] The IAEA's ability to ensure non-proliferation
compliance is hampered by the unwillingness of member
states to expand the agency's inspection mandate and authority. Twenty-two countries that are party to the NPT do not even
have a safeguards agreement with the IAEA, which further

weakens the agency's ability to police the non-proliferation regime.

The IAEA has been criticised for not responding promptly and effectively to instances of non-compliance. The agency has been inconsistent in the way it reports violations in various cases, which Iran has attempted to exploit. The technical and legal interpretation of what constitutes non-compliance is still subject to debate. An immediate way to strengthen the non-proliferation regime, according to former IAEA Deputy Director General Pierre Goldschmidt, would be to clarify the roles of the agency's director general and Board of Governors with regard to the definition and reporting of non-compliance.[2] This would provide the Security Council with a stronger legal basis to act against violators.

Criticisms of the agency are valid but somewhat misguided. The agency is not legally responsible for violations that occur in facilities and programmes that are beyond its purview. So far all known cases of non-compliance have concerned undeclared nuclear facilities and materials. Under standard safeguards, IAEA inspections cannot monitor activities in facilities that have not been declared, even if suspicions may exist. These concerns have led to growing efforts to broaden the scope of inspections and to make them more effective. They have also prompted the governments most opposed to proliferation to apply unilateral political and economic pressures on states that are suspected of prohibited clandestine nuclear activities.

Stronger protocols

In the wake of the Gulf War in 1991, when it was discovered that Iraq had developed a clandestine nuclear-weapons programme, the IAEA developed new inspection standards to strengthen its ability to detect illicit activities. The Additional Protocol to the 1972 Safeguards Agreement was adopted in 1997 to give the IAEA broader access to information and nuclear sites around the world. It has allowed the agency to focus on a more information-driven, country-level approach that increases confidence about the absence of undeclared activity.

So far 128 states have signed the Additional Protocol, but that leaves many that have not done so. This lack of universal adherence weakens efforts to establish more rigorous standards for non-proliferation verification. One way of strengthening compliance would be for supplier states to make acceptance of the Additional Protocol a condition for the receipt of nuclear materials, services and technologies. To sweeten such an arrangement supplier states could also develop a generic export-license system guaranteeing the supply of nuclear fuel to a state as long as it adheres strictly to IAEA non-proliferation obligations.[3]

The report of the independent commission to the IAEA has noted the need to go beyond the measures called for in the Additional Protocol to provide greater confidence that nuclear programmes are entirely peaceful. A more rigorous set of monitoring requirements has been identified as 'Additional Protocol Plus'. These would give the IAEA the right and the obligation to access sites and information related to nuclear-material production technologies, such as centrifuge manufacturing facilities. It would enable the agency to monitor potential weaponisation activities, and to conduct private interviews with individuals who may know about such activities.[4]

Political challenges

The problems at the IAEA are more political than technical. The inspections carried out by the staff secretariat are highly professional and competent, but the Board of Governors has been inconsistent in the political attention it pays to breaches of safeguards agreements. A pivotal question is whether the focus of inspections and subsequent decision-making should be on actions or intentions by the target state. Because of the dual-use character of most nuclear technology and material, actions alone may not provide decisive evidence of potential military diversion (as the Iranian case shows). It is also important to examine the intentions behind the actions. Any attempt to assess intentions, however, inevitably brings in a major dose of politics to a Board selected primarily on the basis of technical competence. Entering the murky waters of politics may be necessary but it complicates the technical role of the agency.[5]

The enforcement of safeguards compliance belongs to the UN Security Council, which can resort to both negative and positive measures at its disposal. According to the IAEA Statute, the Board of Governors is obliged to report instances of non-compliance to the Security Council and General Assembly. The WMD issue has been on the agenda of the Council dozens of times, but it has resulted in concrete action on only seven occasions, six of which have been based on referral from the IAEA.[6] Some commentators have suggested the creation of a separate technical inspectorate directly under the Security Council, but historical experience supports the view that the IAEA should remain the primary 'forensic institution' of the UN in matters of nuclear proliferation, because of its proven technical competence.[7]

Goldschmidt and others have proposed the adoption of generic Security Council resolutions requiring action against states that blatantly violate IAEA safeguard requirements or undermine global non-proliferation norms. The path to such an approach was opened at a previous Council meeting of heads of state in January 1992, when the assembled leaders declared in a consensus statement that the proliferation of WMD is a threat to international peace and security and that the Council should take 'appropriate measures' under Chapter VII of the

UN Charter in the event of violations.[8] Two types of generic resolutions have been suggested. The first would apply in cases where the IAEA reports a finding of noncompliance. The Council would automatically adopt a resolution under Chapter VII requiring the non-compliant state to grant extended access rights to the IAEA. If the director general could not report full compliance within 60 days, a second automatic resolution would follow requiring the state to suspend all enrichment and reprocessing activities. If this were not followed, a third resolution would be adopted suspending military cooperation and the supply of technical equipment until the state became fully compliant. A second type of generic resolution would apply in cases of states withdrawing from the NPT. Under these circumstances all materials and equipment made available to the state under IAEA safeguards agreements would have to be sealed by the agency and removed from the state. If the state refused to comply, the Council would adopt a resolution suspending any military-cooperation agreements and halting the further supply of technical equipment.[9] The Security Council has been reluctant to consider the adoption of automatic sanctions and instead has adopted sets of country-specific resolutions to impose sanctions on Iraq, Iran and North Korea to persuade them to comply with their responsibilities under the NPT.

Resource constraints

The IAEA's responsibilities and burdens in monitoring nuclear facilities have greatly expanded in recent decades. The resources needed to carry out this work have not kept pace, however. From 1984 to 2007, the amount of nuclear material under IAEA safeguards increased tenfold, but the agency's budget for nuclear safeguards until recently has remained stagnant. Modernisation of the agency's scientific and information infrastructure is long overdue. Since the early 1980s, the agency has been subject to zero real growth in funding, with the exception of modest increases in 2003 and 2009. Given the greatly increased responsibilities of the agency, and the even larger obligations that will result from global efforts to establish monitored disarmament, a major boost in IAEA funding is urgently needed. The IAEA safeguards budget is less than that of the police department of the city of Vienna, where the agency is headquartered.[10] In 2009 the agency received a modest budgetary boost of 2.7% above inflation, the first in a series of planned budget increases in the coming years.[11] A strengthened IAEA with greater resources and stronger inspection authority is essential to international non-proliferation and disarmament objectives.

The agency needs additional authority and funding not only to perform the current level of required inspections but to meet the greater demands that will exist in a world where nuclear weapons are being reduced to zero. The agency needs its own world-class research and development facilities so that it can stay abreast of evolving nuclear technologies and utilise the latest achievements in engineering and science. IAEA Deputy Director General Olli Heinonen has pointed out that the expected 'nuclear renaissance' will absorb a growing share of the technical expertise in the field. This means that even if the resources of the IAEA are expanded, there may be a shortage of competent inspectors to perform the technical tasks.[12]

Verification innovations

In discussing future verification strategies, George Perkovich and James Acton have made a useful distinction between 'evolutionary' and 'radical' approaches. The former includes incremental improvements in present IAEA safeguards that would increase the coverage, effectiveness and timeliness of inspections. The latter approach would call for more comprehensive and effective controls and even ownership of the nuclear fuel cycle.[13] Serious progress in nuclear abolition will require both radical and evolutionary approaches, the former building on the latter.

On the evolutionary path, a promising new approach to streamline the agency's inspection mandate is to employ so-called 'safeguards discounts'. These are arrangements in which the agency conducts fewer inspections at less sensitive sites such as power reactors or low-enrichment research facilities, so that it can concentrate its resources on searching for specific indicators of potential nuclear weaponisation activities – such as programmes that have uneconomical facilities-to-reactor ratios, or in countries that have refused to accept the Additional Protocol. The frequency and extensiveness of visits to low-risk facilities could be reduced, in return for more transparency from the operators of these facilities. Under this arrangement the agency would establish small teams of qualified specialists specifically equipped and trained for this purpose. This system could be supplemented with real-time remote monitoring capabilities. The IAEA could then prioritise its safeguards efforts according to the degree of potential proliferation risk, rather than scaling the number of inspections in proportion to the size of the national nuclear programme, as it does now.

One of the important steps in strengthening and streamlining global nuclear safeguards would be delineating as precisely as possible those activities that constitute purely peaceful nuclear-energy production and those that have no purpose other than potential weaponisation. Perkovich has proposed that the G20 take up this task. The goal would be to strengthen the firewall between peaceful and military nuclear uses by identifying and targeting activities that are obviously military-related and that prevent the IAEA from verifying their purpose.[14] This solution would require judgements not only about actions but about intentions, with all the political complications this would entail. A drawback in this proposal is that the G20 is hardly an appropriate body to perform such tasks. It is a loose coalition of governments and has neither executive capacity nor experience in the field of nuclear non-proliferation.

A more radical approach, which would build political confidence among countries in the global South, would be the extension of IAEA safeguards to the production facilities of the NWS. This idea has been resolutely rejected by nuclear-weapons states in the past, and although it remains unlikely it might be feasible in the future as a concession by the United States and the other NWS to encourage support for global disarmament efforts. The report of the independent commission on the role of the IAEA observed that 'it would be logical, as disarmament proceeds, for states to give the Agency a central role in monitoring the huge stockpiles of fissile materials that would be freed from nuclear weapons programs'.[15] Under the US–Russia–IAEA Trilateral Initiative, technologies, procedures and model agreements have already been developed for the IAEA to monitor these stockpiles without compromising sensitive information.

The United States, Russia or other nuclear powers could begin to open their facilities to IAEA monitoring without risk to their security. Such an agreement would represent a significant good-faith gesture towards establishing a more equitable, non-discriminatory disarmament and non-proliferation regime. Precedents exist for intrusive on-site external inspections in the verification protocols that the United States accepted in the INF and START treaties. Providing similar access to a highly professional and neutral monitoring body like the IAEA should pose no difficulties from a security perspective. As Scott Sagan points out, Article IV of the NPT refers to 'all the Parties to the

Treaty', implying that safeguard requirements apply to NWS and NNWS alike. By beginning to place nuclear plants and enrichment and reprocessing facilities under IAEA safeguards, Sagan suggests, the NWS could demonstrate their commitment to disarmament and establish best practices.[16]

It is clear that progress towards nuclear zero will require more intrusive methods of verification. The closer the world moves towards nuclear zero, the greater the degree of transparency and openness that will be required of all governments. The need to investigate and disclose undeclared nuclear capabilities will be especially difficult to accept for more closed societies. For these states the process of disarmament will probably clash more than once with a narrow interpretation of the principle of national sovereignty. The sharing of relevant technical information on nuclear activities is already a contested ground in international relations and will likely become more so in the future.

Multinationalising the fuel cycle

Gaining control over the nuclear fuel cycle remains a critically important but unresolved challenge. The task will become more difficult if the anticipated renaissance of nuclear industry leads to a multiplication of enrichment and reprocessing facilities. The expansion of such facilities in regions of potential conflict, such as South Asia and the Middle East, poses special security risks.

Enrichment facilities are currently operating in the United States, Russia, China, Canada and several European countries. India and Pakistan enrich uranium on a small scale, and in 2006 Brazil opened a new centrifuge facility at its Resende nuclear plant. Iran, of course, has developed a disputed enrichment programme. Israel, North Korea and South Africa are also suspected of enriching uranium.[17]

Proposals for addressing the fuel cycle problem include various options for guaranteeing the supply of nuclear materials through Multilateral Nuclear Agreements (MNA), which are multinational production and supply arrangements. The core principle of MNA is that all uranium enrichment and plutonium separation should be conducted in multinational facilities under stringent safeguards. The report of the independent commission to the IAEA recommended the promotion of a trend towards increasing the international or multilateral ownership and control of enrichment and reprocessing worldwide.[18] A related proposal is establishing a global register of stocks of plutonium and highly enriched uranium. UN Security Council Resolution 1887 included a provision encouraging 'multilateral approaches to the nuclear fuel cycle, including assurances of fuel supply'.[19]

Multinationalisation makes great sense in economic terms. Building and operating fuel-cycle facilities is an enormously expensive and complex operation. The construction of large-scale multinational facilities in a limited number of locations would be far less expensive for the countries involved than building separate facilities. Russia has established the International Uranium Enrichment Center at Angarsk as a potential source of nuclear fuel to reactors around the world. The Nuclear Threat Initiative, a private US organisation, has pledged $50 million towards the creation of an IAEA-owned reserve of low-enriched uranium, and the United States, the European Union, UAE, Norway and Kuwait have collectively pledged an additional $100m.

The proposals for multinational nuclear production have largely fallen on deaf ears in important parts of the global South. Several countries belonging to the Non-Aligned Movement (NAM), which do not ally themselves to any great power, have expressed concerns that they would be forced to 'surrender' their fuel-production rights and would be subject to the political whims of supplier states and organisations. They fear that a supplier cartel managed by the major nuclear powers would restrict their access to nuclear technology. Acquiring an indigenous nuclear industry is seen by some post-colonial states as an essential goal of economic development, a matter of national pride and a symbol of self-determination. The reluctance of non-nuclear states is fed by resentment over the discriminatory features of the non-proliferation regime. These fears are accentuated by the fact that the growing global demand for nuclear reactors may create fuel shortages. Some states are concerned that oligopolistic vendors would favour more developed and stable countries, further discriminating against developing countries.

In February 2004 President George W. Bush called for a ban on the sale of nuclear-enrichment and processing equipment to countries that do not already have such facilities. He proposed that nuclear exporters ensure access to reactor fuel for states without production capacity, provided these states renounce the right to enrichment and reprocessing. Whatever the merits, or lack thereof, of Bush's proposal, the fact that it came in the wake of the invasion of Iraq convinced many that it was simply another form of unilateralism intended to confer permanent advantage on the nuclear-weapons states. Bush's proposal was criticised as discriminatory and subsequently dropped by US officials.

IAEA Director General Mohamed ElBaradei offered a different proposal. His plan included restrictions on the processing of weapons-usable material in civilian nuclear programmes, agreement to limit such operations exclusively to facilities under multinational control, the development of nuclear-energy systems that are designed to be proliferation resistant and multinational approaches to the management and disposable of spent fuel and radioactive waste.[20] ElBaradei's proposal avoided some of the discriminatory features of the Bush plan, but it has also faced scepticism from countries in the global South.

As the IAEA Expert Group on these issues concluded in its 2005 report, multinational nuclear fuel mechanisms are only conceivable on a non-discriminatory basis. This would require advanced states with existing nuclear-production plants to integrate their capabilities into the proposed multi-lateral arrangements. This seems to be the only feasible way of overcoming resistance in the global South to discriminatory approaches. The development of regional nuclear regulatory agencies modeled after the European Atomic Energy Community (EURATOM), but with greater operational and production capability, might be a step in this direction. Such agencies would manage nuclear production in their region, cooperating fully with IAEA safeguards, to guarantee nuclear fuel for member states while assuring the peaceful character of production activities. Such regional arrangements would be particularly important in potential conflict zones.

EU policies

The security strategy of the European Union (EU), adopted in December 2003, defines nuclear proliferation as one of the four key threats to European security. Its operational strategy against the proliferation of WMD was formulated in 2004. The EU does not, of course, have its own nuclear weapons strategy, but two of its member states, France and the United Kingdom, do. For this reason the activities of the Union have focused on cementing cooperation between member states for more effective global governance in non-proliferation efforts and for controlling exports of proliferation-sensitive materials. A smaller coalition of member states has exerted leadership in attempting to persuade Iran to give up its possible quest for nuclear-weapons capability. Since 2003, the EU has adopted more than 20 Joint Actions to promote international goals of nuclear non-proliferation.[21] The EU and its member states are active supporters of the IAEA and have consistently advocated the strengthening of its safeguards system and the establishment of an international fuel bank under its auspices.

The EU emphasis is on compliance with multilateral treaties and agreements such as the NPT. This approach facilitates consensus within NATO, since the United States also supports treaty compliance. The means of implementing these obligations include stronger and internationally coordinated export controls among EU member states, cooperative threat-reduction programmes, the use of political and economic inducements to encourage compliance by EU member states and governments receiving EU assistance, the interdiction of illegal weapons trafficking, and participation in UN sanctions and other multilateral enforcement measures. The Union also provides substantial material resources to support peace-building activities in crisis-ridden regions. Its activities for conflict resolution, crisis management and humanitarian assistance contribute to regional peace and stability that can underpin efforts at nuclear disarmament.

Cooperative policy tools

A broad consensus exists on key elements of a cooperative international strategy against nuclear terrorism and proliferation. These elements are: securing all weapons-usable materials against theft or diversion; ending the production of these materials; banning the use of these materials in civilian research facilities, power-production reactors and naval vessels; and eliminating the large surplus stockpiles of these materials held by the United States, Russia and other nations. Many of these programmes are now in place in the United States, the EU and other regions. Progress in these non-proliferation efforts can contribute to nuclear abolition. The strengthening of non-proliferation controls builds the foundation for achieving disarmament. In fact, it would be unrealistic to expect the NWS to reduce significantly their nuclear arsenals without stronger non-proliferation controls.

The United States has provided important leadership in many of these technical programmes, although there are concerns that the programmes are not adequately funded and are not considered sufficiently urgent by legislators and policy-makers. The 9/11 Commission, which was set up to investigate the circumstances surrounding the terrorist attacks on New York and Washington, gave the US government failing grades in the area of securing nuclear materials to prevent terror-ist nuclear strikes. The chairman of the commission, former New Jersey Governor Thomas Kean, questioned why securing nuclear materials was not a greater national security priority.[22] Notwithstanding such criticisms, very substantial technical programmes are in place to strengthen global non-proliferation efforts.

The Cooperative Threat Reduction Programme (CTR) is one of the most extensive and well established of these efforts. Its goal has been to secure and dismantle nuclear weapons and materi-als in the former Soviet Union. Created in 1992 at the initiative of US Senators Sam Nunn and Richard Lugar, the programme helps to eliminate the facilities, technology and materials used to produce nuclear, chemical and biological weapons. It has operated primarily in Russia, Azerbaijan, Georgia, Kazakhstan, Ukraine and Uzbekistan. Its current budget is $404m per year, which is used to dismantle nuclear facilities, upgrade security at nuclear sites and provide compensation for nuclear scien-tists and technicians. Since its implementation, the CTR has deactivated over 7,500 warheads, destroyed 906 nuclear air-to-surface missiles and upgraded security at 24 nuclear-weapons storage facilities. By the time the programme is completed in 2012, a total of 8,452 warheads are expected to have been deactivated.[23]

The United States and Russia have agreed to cooperate in the disposal of 68 metric tons of weapons-grade plutonium. Half of this, enough to produce more than 4,000 bombs, will be converted to nuclear fuel at the US Savannah River Site.[24] The United States and Russia are also working together in the so-called Megatons to Megawatts Program. The United States has purchased 500 metric tons of highly enriched uranium, converting three-quarters of it into fuel for nuclear power reactors.[25] Nuclear fuel from this programme is now being used to produce approximately 10% of the electricity generated in the United States.[26] These have been positive steps, but Nunn and others have urged a larger effort and a more urgent timeline for completing the job of securing nuclear materials.

In 2004 the US Department of Energy established the Global Threat Reduction Initiative (GTRI), which integrated and upgraded efforts to secure and remove highly enriched uranium (HEU) from research reactors and civilian nuclear facilities around the world. The GTRI has worked to convert civilian reactors from using HEU to low-enriched uranium (LEU) in locations across Europe and the United States, and at facilities in China, Libya and South Africa. By the beginning of 2009, GTRI had overseen the removal of over 1,000kg of highly enriched uranium, enough to produce more than 40 nuclear bombs. The GTRI has also removed a total of 145kg of 'gap material', nuclear material not covered by the CTR or other programmes.[27] The initiative's funding has increased steadily over the past several years from a budget of $69.5m in 2004 to $395m in the original 2009 appropriation, with one-third of the 2009 budget devoted to removing nuclear material of Russian origin.[28] GTRI's annual budget is expected to increase to more than $1 billion by fiscal year 2014,[29] greatly expanding the Department of Energy's ability to convert, remove or protect sensitive nuclear material across the globe. This initiative has helped reduce the risk of HEU falling into the hands of potential aggressors. CTR and GTRI have helped to limit the potential spread of weapons-building materials and capacity.

In 2004 the UN Security Council adopted Resolution 1540 obliging all UN member states not to provide any support to non-state actors related to the development or transfer of nuclear weapons and other means of mass destruction. An important part of the resolution is the decision that illicit traffic in WMD constitutes a threat to international peace and security. This facilitates the application of the enforcement instruments available in Chapter VII of the UN Charter. The resolution requires states to adopt laws and national enforcement measures to prevent proliferation activities by non-state actors. The Security Council committee and expert group created to enforce the resolution have worked with states to enhance implementation of the resolution. Their primary emphasis has been on building an international consensus for urgent attention to this problem. They have also identified the need to provide greater capacity-building assistance for the many states that do not yet have sufficient legal and administrative machinery to enforce non-proliferation mandates.

In 2003 the United States initiated the Proliferation Security Initiative (PSI) to enlist the cooperation of 95 countries in efforts to prevent illegal trafficking in weapons components and materials.[30] The most important feature of the programme is the policy of searching and interdicting vessels that are suspected of engaging in illegal weapons trafficking. In its first year of operation the PSI led to at least 11 interdictions of goods related to nuclear and ballistic-missile programmes.[31] Since then, US State Department officials have claimed several successful interdictions, but offered few specific details due to the 'confidential nature of interdictions conducted by PSI partners'.[32]

The PSI was not created as a treaty-based programme, and thus lacks an international legal foundation. As a result some states have been reluctant to participate fully. Important littoral states such as China, Indonesia and Malaysia are wary of the initiative. On the other hand, nine of the major flag-of-convenience countries, including Cyprus, Liberia and Panama, which collectively register more than one-half of the world's largest cargo ships, have entered into formal ship-boarding agreements with the US, which strengthens international capabilities to interdict illicit cargo.[33]

The legal basis of the PSI was strengthened by Resolution 1540, and by the UN's 2005 Convention for the Suppression of Unlawful Actions Against the Safety of Maritime Navigation (SUA), which defines proliferation-related activity as unlawful. Operational dimensions of the PSI, specifically the interdiction of weapons trafficking, were incorporated into Resolution 1874 (2009), which is directed at preventing North Korea from selling arms or obtaining materials or assistance that would aid the expansion of its weapons programmes. Resolution 1874 authorises UN member states to inspect cargo located within their territories bound to or from North Korea. States are authorised, with the consent of the flag state, to inspect vessels suspected of transporting cargo relating to North Korea's weapons programmes.[34]

The incorporation of these search and seizure provisions into a binding Security Council resolution strengthens the legal foundations of the PSI, at least in relation to the North Korea case. The confiscation of North Korean arms by the UAE and

Thailand in August and December 2009, respectively, were early indications of the resolution's impact.[35] Resolution 1874 could set a precedent for a subsequent Security Council resolution or UN agreement that would universalise the PSI and strengthen its legal and political legitimacy.

The operational strength of the PSI is due to its informal and flexible nature; sovereign states share information voluntarily and the core members are responsible for interdictions. On the other hand, the PSI is seen by some critics as a US tool. Amitai Etzioni claims, unfairly, that it 'acts as a single standing global antiproliferation force led by one nation, with a rotating cast of volunteers joining the patrols and raids'.[36] The efficiency of the PSI could be enhanced by greater efforts to strengthen its foundations in binding international law.

CTBT and non-proliferation

The most important step in building non-proliferation cooperation would be universal ratification and entry into force of the Comprehensive Test-Ban Treaty (CTBT). A legal ban on testing and completion of the treaty's robust verification regime are vital to achieving not only NPT objectives but nuclear disarmament in general. The United States and Russia have maintained a voluntary moratorium on nuclear testing since the early 1990s, and neither country has plans to conduct tests in the future. The UK, France and China also halted testing in the 1990s. More than 180 states have signed the test-ban treaty and 152 have ratified it, but there are important hold-outs, including the United States, where the Senate rejected ratification in 1999; China, which also has signed but not ratified; and India, which has refused even to sign the treaty. Achieving the full support of these and other hold-out states is currently high on the international policy agenda. Security Council Resolution 1887 (2009) urged all states to ratify and implement the treaty.

US ratification of the CTBT would be the single most important step for universalising the NPT. Approval is not assured in the US Senate, however, where deep political disagreements remain on the verifiability of the treaty, the reliability of the US stockpile and its impact on US national security.[37]

Banning nuclear tests directly advances non-proliferation. Without the ability to conduct test explosions, states seeking to build the bomb may face uncertainty regarding the reliability and effectiveness of their weapons. India, Pakistan and North Korea conducted tests in their quests to develop nuclear weapons. Israel and South Africa, on the other hand, may have built the bomb without testing, although a double flash observed by a US satellite in the Indian Ocean in 1979 is seen by some as evidence of a joint test.[38] Military planners prefer the technical assurances of viability that only testing can provide. Testing programmes enable aspiring nuclear powers to improve and miniaturise warhead designs for deployment on ballistic missiles and possible multiple-warhead systems. By prohibiting this, the CTBT helps block new nuclear threats from emerging, thereby enhancing global security.

Critics question whether a comprehensive test ban can be verified, but in recent years monitoring systems and detection technology have reached advanced states of reliability, in part because of the continuing efforts of the Comprehensive Test-Ban Treaty Organisation (CTBTO), which was established in 1997. CTBTO has an International Monitoring System (IMS) of more than 300 seismic detection and monitoring stations all over the world. The United States and other member states can also monitor CTBT compliance with their own, highly sophisticated satellites and other intelligence means. Thousands of high-quality civilian seismic stations around the world provide further detection capabilities.

This extensive international detection network proved its worth when North Korea conducted its first nuclear-weapons test explosion in October 2006. The global network of sensors easily detected Pyongyang's relatively low-yield (0.6 kiloton) blast. Most nuclear tests are considerably larger. The explosion was promptly detected and identified from signals recorded at 31 seismic stations in Asia, Australia, Europe and North America, including 22 IMS stations.[39] No nuclear explosion of military significance can escape global detection.

The US Senate could play a constructive role in advancing non-proliferation and disarmament by agreeing to ratification of the CTBT. US action could set in motion a pattern of reciprocating ratification action by the hold-out states that would have a significant positive impact on non-proliferation dynamics and perhaps in reducing regional tensions. There is no guarantee that this would occur, of course, given the political obstacles in each state, but no progress with the hold-outs will be possible if Washington does not act. In that sense US ratification is a necessary but not sufficient catalyst for encouraging further ratification. It may be worthwhile, nonetheless, to consider the potential positive ramifications. Indonesia has said it will ratify when the US does, and China has hinted at the same. This would in turn increase pressure on India to ratify. Pakistan would follow suit. US ratification and encouragement might also help to persuade Israel to ratify. Egypt, which has said it will not ratify unless Israel joins the NPT as a non-nuclear weapons state, might be encouraged to modify its view and ratify the treaty as well.

This envisioned cascade of ratification – far more desirable than the 'cascade of proliferation' so many analysts fear – would help to bolster the credibility and value of mutual disarmament and could set a precedent for subsequent disarmament agreements. The same pattern might be followed with agreements banning all production of weapons-grade fissile material and strengthening inspection and verification protocols. The United States and Russia would lead the way, inviting China to join, along with France and the United Kingdom, followed by efforts to encourage the support of India, Pakistan and Israel. Ultimately, the ratification of the CTBT and conclusion of a fissile material cut-off treaty should belong to the disarmament obligations assumed by the NWS under Article VI of the NPT.

Conclusion

The road towards nuclear zero will be long and arduous, with many detours and reversals along the way. Reaching that goal will require a step-by-step process that proceeds steadily towards the ultimate destination. Nunn has used the metaphor of climbing a mountain.[40] The goal of a world without nuclear weapons can be likened to the peak of a very tall mountain. It is not fully visible from the base, and it is tempting to think that the climb is impossible. Yet paths are visible, and they can lead to higher ground where other paths will appear. Each advance towards the summit reveals new challenges and obstacles, but also new possibilities for reaching the top. The way towards the peak of disarmament is through the paths of more effective non-proliferation policy – ironclad verification and monitoring systems, international control of the nuclear fuel cycle and greater political cooperation in reducing threats and banning nuclear tests. These steps will create safer foundations for contemporary global security while smoothing the journey towards nuclear disarmament in the future.

CHAPTER EIGHT

Nuclear Zero and Beyond

Some analysts still believe that disarmament is a form of surrender. They fear that the elimination of nuclear weapons would expose nations to aggression and intimidation. Henry Kissinger once wrote that a policy of no first use of nuclear weapons 'would leave us psychologically naked'.[1] Kissinger has changed his mind and now sees disarmament as part of the fabric of international security. Progressive denuclearisation is fully compatible with an enlightened political realism. Nations that give up the bomb or weapons programmes – as Ukraine, South Africa and Brazil have done – gain in security and global standing. Those that seek this capability – such as North Korea and Iran – are international pariahs. The United States and Russia have slashed nuclear arsenals once considered untouchable and are arguably more secure as a result. Arms reduction and disarmament are means of increasing security, not reducing it.

There are various stages of disarmament, and each has different security implications. The dynamics of deterrence change as nuclear weapons diminish towards zero, but the core elements of power balancing and competition among nations remain and can be addressed through non-nuclear means. At each stage in the disarmament process – minimum deterrence, virtual arsenals, nuclear prohibition, weaponless deterrence – strategies are available for maintaining and enhancing security and guarding against cheating or nuclear break-out. Security is never absolute, and any alternative security system will contain risks. Mutual vulnerability is not a choice, as a Council on Foreign Relations task force recently observed, but a fact that needs to be managed.[2] This requires a focus on enhancing strategic stability and reducing nuclear dangers, while applying robust means to address potential security threats.

Minimum deterrence and the nuclear 'vantage point'

As nations reduce nuclear arsenals they will reach a mutual posture of minimum deterrence that has been described as the strategic 'vantage point'. This is a point short of nuclear zero where states may wish to pause on the way down. It is a policy space far below the large arsenals that exist today that does not require states to abandon their deployed nuclear weapons altogether. David Holloway and James E. Goodby have described this as an 'interim option' on the way towards nuclear zero, a policy goal that would enable states to make a strategic assessment as to whether conditions are ripe for moving ahead to the final stages of eliminating the last deployed nuclear weapons.[3] The number of permitted weapons and the characteristics of the vantage point would need to be carefully defined and agreed. Holloway et al., have suggested a level of 50–100 total warheads.[4] The usual minimum deterrence estimate is 100–200 weapons. If the United States and Russia could agree to a mutual reduction to this level, their arsenals would be equivalent to those of China, the United Kingdom and France. The nuclear powers recognised by the NPT would then be in a position to establish the conditions for moving with with other nuclear-weapons states nearer to zero.

The path from today's world of massive nuclear arsenals to nuclear zero will be a long one, and for most of that journey it will not be necessary for states to decide definitively whether they intend to remain at the vantage point of minimum deterrence or proceed to zero. The steps required to get to the minimum point are the same as those required to reach zero. They are all part of what George Perkovich has defined as a 'danger minimisation strategy', a range of actions and policies that seek to 'minimize the roles, numbers, and launch-edginess of nuclear weapons'.[5] It is not necessary to know and decide all the details of the vantage point in the early stages of the journey. As the United States and Russia achieve progress towards minimum deterrence, they will gain confidence and knowledge in whether and how to proceed towards zero. The steps along the way, meanwhile, will enhance global security and make the world a safer and more equitable place.[6]

Some have argued that deterrence is weakened and unstable at low numbers. This is the so-called 'instability of small numbers' problem. Thomas Schelling and Charles Glaser have argued that the danger of nuclear-weapons use may increase as states reduce towards zero. This is a legitimate concern, since the value of a small arsenal increases as overall numbers diminish, which may increase the temptation to seek an advantage through nuclear break-out.[7] Historical experience suggests, however, that states can maintain relatively stable deterrence relations at minimum force levels. China has managed to maintain its nuclear deterrent with relatively low numbers, even in a very asymmetrical relationship vis-à-vis the huge arsenals of Russia and the United States. Russia today has a very large numerical superiority over the United States and NATO in short-range nuclear weapons, but this disparity does not undermine deterrence or confer any strategic advantages to Russia. India and Pakistan are in a conflict-prone relationship and possess relatively low numbers, and yet are assumed to be in a mutual deterrent posture. As Perkovich writes, 'there is plenty of experience around the world since 1945 to suggest that deterrence and stability can be maintained with low numbers of nuclear weapons'. Arms-control measures and enhanced transparency procedures can be developed to augment that stability at lower numbers.[8] Deterrence relationships persist at the minimum level as they do all along the path to zero.

Virtual Deterrence

Related to the idea of minimal deterrence is the concept of virtual nuclear arsenals (VNA), the partial dismantlement of nuclear weapons through the removal of warheads from launch vehicles. As states reach the vantage point and decide to proceed towards zero, they could agree to a process of separating warheads from launch vehicles. Michael Mazarr writes, 'VNAs aim to achieve some of the advantages of complete nuclear disarmament, removing all nuclear weapons from day-to-day operational status and thereby seeking to push them to the margins of world politics, while allowing current nuclear powers to retain some of the core missions' for these forces.[9] The components of strategic arsenals would remain – missiles, guidance sets, fissile material, warheads – which could be reassembled within a designated time. The scheduled time for reassembly could be defined with some precision and might be as short as a few days or weeks.

Former CIA Director and retired Admiral Stansfield Turner proposed a similar idea. His 'strategic escrow' plan would remove US warheads from missiles and place them in designated hardened storage sites at a fixed distance, perhaps 320km, from launchers.[10] Other states would be encouraged to follow the US lead. The goal would be to establish a practice, without the requirement of lengthy multilateral negotiations, in which all nuclear-weapons states agree to separate warheads from launchers and place them in internationally supervised storage sites at a fixed distance from launchers. A limit would be established of no more than 200 warheads and accompanying launchers for each state. A system of monitored security protection and international inspection would be established to guard against attempts to steal the warheads and to provide early warning of any attempt to reconstitute weapons by mating warheads to launch vehicles.[11]

The foundation of the virtual nuclear-deterrence concept is the separation of warheads from launchers. This is the minimum necessary step for shifting from actual to virtual arsenals, writes Mazarr.[12] Nuclear weapons would be disassembled and no longer deployed. Deterrence would remain, however, based on the understanding that states would have the capacity and authority to reassemble and redeploy within a defined period of time. In this context, and in relation to the concept of weaponless deterrence, the time factor becomes an element of security. Deterrence becomes a function not only of weapons capabilities but of the length of time required for reassembling or reconstituting weapons components. As the disarmament process becomes more thorough, evolving from virtual arsenals to nuclear abolition and then to weaponless deterrence based on reconstitution capacity, the time required to reintroduce nuclear weapons lengthens. The goal is always to increase that time, to lessen the nuclear danger and further diminish the role of nuclear weapons. The more thorough the disarmament process, the longer the time required for nuclear reconstitution.

Virtual or weaponless deterrence reduces the inequalities in the nuclear balance of power. As the NWS evolve towards a stage of potential rather than actual nuclear-weapons capability, their status will begin to resemble that of the many other states that have the capacity to build nuclear weapons but choose not to do so. For all states the question will become not whether they could have nuclear weapons, but rather how long it would take to create them. The key criterion is the cushion of time between a given stage of nuclear technology and deployed nuclear weapons.[13] This broad potential for nuclear capability constitutes a general deterrent effect, involving not only current and former nuclear-weapons states but dozens of other countries that could weaponise if they so choose. This general deterrent capability would act collectively as a counterweight to would-be aggressors and nuclear cheaters.

With virtual arsenals the value of nuclear weapons diminishes.[14] As the number of ready-to-deploy nuclear weapons reaches zero, further stages of disarmament become possible. Moving beyond VNA to a less immediate and more ethereal form of deterrence will take additional multilateral agreements that are likely to be reached in incremental stages. Nuclear-weapons states could steadily reduce the number of warheads kept in storage and disassembly as they move towards the complete dismantling of all nuclear weapons and their components. At the end of the process, nuclear knowledge and the ability to reassemble dispersed components would be all that remains, and would constitute the final form of deterrence.

Missile defences: from obstacle to solution

The perceived need for missile defences has been an obstacle to reaching agreement on nuclear reductions and disarmament. Differences over this issue prevented Presidents Ronald Reagan and Mikhail Gorbachev from reaching a historic agreement to eliminate nuclear weapons at Reykjavik in 1986. The question remains an important one today, and has become more urgent as the US government has started to deploy such systems. So far the technical capabilities of missile defence systems lag far behind their declared potential. The ability to shoot down ballistic missiles and counter the threat from cruise missiles has not been proven, despite the expenditure of hundreds of billions of dollars in missile defence development programmes in recent decades. These programmes have generated more political controversy than actual protection against missiles.

Nonetheless, the trend towards missile defences is accelerating. Defensive systems are favoured in Washington in part because they offer the promise of re-establishing US superiority in conventional weaponry and military technology, which is threatened by proliferation. Missile-defence programmes also provide a means of reinforcing alliance and security relationships that have weakened with the rise of multipolarity.[15] On the other hand missile-defence plans exacerbate various security dilemmas within alliances.

Many policymakers and analysts over the decades have worried about the destabilising character of missile defences. These concerns persist today. Russia and China fear that a fully developed US missile-defence system could neutralise their retaliatory capabilities, and that the combination of effective missile defences and continued large-scale US strategic nuclear deployments would constitute a first-strike threat. Russia has objected strenuously to proposed missile-defence deployments in Poland and the Czech Republic. During the Bush administration US–Russia differences over the issue had detrimental impacts on bilateral relations and impeded cooperation on other issues.

As part of its efforts to improve relations with Russia, the Obama administration redirected plans to deploy a radar system in the Czech Republic and ten interceptor missiles in Poland. This is not to say that the United States has given up the idea of missile-defence deployment, however. The current plan is to place radar sites closer to Iranian borders and to deploy interceptors on ships in the Black and Baltic Seas. These moves may be politically astute, but they do not remove the ongoing surge towards missile defences that would include the deployment of *Patriot* missiles in Poland and the continuing development of Japanese missile-defence systems.

In practical terms, this means that the destabilising impacts of missile defence will continue. Russia will not be willing to reduce to low numbers of nuclear weapons without assurances of limitations on missile defences. China also will be reluctant to reduce its relatively small nuclear arsenal if it fears that missile defences could neutralise a substantial part of its deterrent capability. A solution to the conundrum will be necessary to achieve progress towards nuclear zero.

Return to Reykjavik

The answer may lie in revisiting the ideas and formulations discussed by Reagan and Gorbachev at Hofdi House in Reykjavik. Reagan had shocked the security establishment in 1983 when he proposed a Strategic Defense Initiative that would render nuclear weapons 'impotent and obsolete'. Once missile defences were in place, he believed, it would be possible to 'eliminate the weapons themselves'. Reagan further shocked the security establishment a few days later when he announced his willingness to share missile defences with the Soviet Union. Once the two countries were defended, he asserted, they could do away with their missiles.

Reagan envisioned missile defences as protection against cheating in a world where nuclear weapons had been eliminated. When offensive arsenals have been reduced to zero, and the principal remaining nuclear danger is the threat of cheating, the mission of missile defence becomes more feasible. In this

scenario, a defensive system would face only a small and technologically immature missile force that a pariah regime might
assemble in secret. This more limited mission became Reagan's
principal rationale for missile defences. As Jonathan Schell
observes, Reagan was thereby 'addressing the most frequently
made and most potent objection to nuclear abolition: that if it
were ever accomplished, the world might be held hostage by a
cheater suddenly in possession of a nuclear monopoly and so
capable of forcing the world to bow to its will'.[16]

At Reykjavik these issues were at the centre of the negotiations. While agreement was not reached, critically important
principles were established that yet could serve as the foundation for a breakthrough in achieving nuclear disarmament.[17]
Gorbachev began the summit with proposals for a 50% reduction in strategic nuclear weapons and the elimination of all
intermediate-range nuclear missiles, but he conditioned these cuts
on restricting the Strategic Defense Initiative (SDI) to the labora-
tory for ten years. Reagan countered by asking why Gorbachev
wanted to restrict defences that 'would make the elimination of
nuclear weapons possible'.[18] In response to the concern that SDI
would give the United States a first-strike advantage, Reagan
again promised to share SDI technology and stated: 'We are
proposing a treaty that would require the elimination of ballistic
missiles before SDI is deployed, therefore a first strike would
not be possible'. Reagan's statement that SDI deployment could
come after the elimination of nuclear missiles was an important
conceptual point that few observers have noted.

On the second day the two leaders seemed to compete with
each other in a dizzying exchange of proposals to eliminate all
nuclear weapons, not just ballistic missiles but cruise missiles,
battlefield weapons and sub-launched weapons, short- and long
-range weapons alike – all set to be thrown, in Schell's words,
'onto the great bonfire of nuclear weapons that now seemed to

be in preparation'. Reagan returned to the question of missile defences and asked how SDI could be 'synchronized with our shared goals of eliminating ballistic missiles'. At a crucial point in the conversation Secretary of State George Shultz asked Gorbachev if withdrawal from the Anti-Ballistic Missile Treaty would be permitted after strategic abolition. Gorbachev answered that it would. This affirmed the very point Reagan had emphasised the day before, that SDI deployment could proceed after nuclear abolition. Agreement was within reach on a formulation for combining abolition and defences. The two sides could not abandon their previous positions, however, and the summit ended in disagreement, although several of the proposals discussed there, including the elimination of all intermediate-range nuclear forces and sharp reductions in strategic nuclear weapons, subsequently came to fruition.

A creative solution to the missile defence conundrum might be achieved by returning to the Reykjavik formula: a commitment to shared defences as a necessary assurance in a world of zero nuclear weapons, with missile defences deployed after nuclear weapons are eliminated. The way to proceed, according to Perkovich, is to 'accept limits on ballistic missile defenses in the near term in order to facilitate multilateral reductions in nuclear arms, and meanwhile to promote cooperation in research, development and potential operations of defenses as states agree to work jointly towards nuclear disarmament'.[19] Under this scenario, nations moving to a future without nuclear weapons would have the option of relying on missile defences as an extra reassurance and protection against cheating and nuclear break-out.

'The knowledge' as deterrent

It is obvious that nuclear weapons cannot be uninvented. This is often used as an argument for why nuclear weapons cannot be eliminated, but it may be the very fact that enables abolition to occur. The prospect that these weapons could be reconstituted after they have been abolished provides a form of deterrence, a weaponless deterrence in which the knowledge of how to make the bomb rather than the bomb itself becomes the basis of security. Even at the stage of nuclear zero, when no nuclear weapons remain, deterrence would continue to function. The knowledge, tools and materials for building the bomb would remain, and therefore the fact that they could be reconstituted would serve as a deterrent.

The concept of weaponless deterrence has existed since the beginning of the atomic age. The Acheson–Lilienthal Report in 1946 outlined a plan for eliminating atomic weapons and creating an international Atomic Development Authority that would own and control fissile materials within states. The report was criticised for lacking an enforcement mechanism, but the authors were not indifferent to the necessity of responding to possible violations. Rather than suggesting that military force be applied against cheaters, as was proposed in the subsequent Baruch Plan, the Acheson–Lilienthal Report relied on the possibility of reconstitution.

It is not thought that the Atomic Development Authority could protect its plants by military force from the overwhelming power of the nation in which they were situated. Some United Nations military guard may be desirable, but at most, such a force could be little more than a token. The real protection would lie in the fact that if any nation seized the plants or the stockpiles that were situated in its territory, other nations would have similar facilities and materials situated within their own borders so that the act of seizure need not place them at a disadvantage. Protection against possible violators, according to the report, would lie in the ability of national governments to reconstitute their nuclear capability.

Schell focused on this phenomenon in his 1984 book *The Abolition*. As nuclear reductions proceed, Schell wrote, 'the capacity for retaliation would consist less and less of the possession of weapons and more and more of the capacity for rebuilding them, until, at the level of zero, that capacity would be all'. Nuclear zero in this understanding is less an absolute endpoint than a set of conditions, stages of zero, 'in which the key issue is no longer the number of weapons in existence but the extent of the capacity and the level of readiness' for rebuilding.[20] In a March 2009 speech at Yale University Schell emphasised the centrality of what he called 'The Knowledge' as the basis for deterrence in a world without nuclear weapons. This approach 'capitalises on the danger that radiates from nuclear know-how even in the absence of the hardware. Yes, that know-how is the basis for cheating on the agreement, but it is also the basis for a response, keeping deterrence intact.'[21]

The concept of virtual deterrence or nuclear reconstitution is closely related to the phenomenon of nuclear hedging. This is a strategy adopted by some states for maintaining an option for the rapid acquisition of nuclear weapons should that become necessary, but not actually preparing this capability. Japan's case is often suggested as an example of nuclear hedging. Although a champion of non-proliferation and disarmament, Japan nonetheless has a highly advanced nuclear industry and conceivably possesses all the technology that would be needed for building nuclear weapons quickly.

Nuclear hedging is also the approach adopted by states that have decided to abandon previous nuclear-weapons programmes. Ariel Levite has observed, 'nuclear hedging appears to have played a critical role in facilitating nuclear reversal in practically every case under examination'.[22] In several of the states, the abandonment of weapons programmes has been accompanied by increased investment in peaceful nuclear energy. These investments were designed in part to facilitate nuclear hedging.[23] The strategy of maintaining a hedge capacity, even after a state has formally decided to forego nuclear weapons acquisition, provides a form of weaponless deterrence. The latent deterrence posture that hedging provides is a form of security against potential aggression and a means of leverage in dealing with powerful states such as the United States.

James E. Goodby and Sydney D. Drell of the Hoover Institution at Stanford University recently examined the technical and political considerations that would be required for operationalising the concept of weaponless deterrence. In reviewing what they term 'end-state issues' for a world without nuclear weapons, Goodby and Drell explore the requirements and procedures that would allow nations to end their reliance on deployed nuclear weapons ready for prompt launch and move instead towards a posture in which they are 'months away from being able to take such a fateful action'.[24] A major task in negotiating a ban on deployed nuclear weapons would be defining the permissible states of readiness for reconstituting weapons and delivery systems. This would require establishing 'parameters for limiting a virtual or latent nuclear weapons capability that will be acceptable to both the most and least advanced nuclear nations'.[25] Negotiating the exact terms and conditions for such infrastructure preservation programmes would be a major task of diplomacy in the final stages of reaching agreement on the elimination of deployed nuclear weapons.

Weapons labs in the nuclear-capable states will play a vital role in managing this threat reduction process. To them will fall the responsibility of ensuring that shrinking nuclear arsenals remain 'safe, secure and reliable', and in the end state itself, that nations retain 'the ability to reconstitute a force if necessary'.[26] This will involve the maintenance of active technical and scientific infrastructure programmes, which will engage in specifically delineated and monitored activities to sustain reconstitution capacity. In the United States this might mean transforming the Stockpile Stewardship and Management Program into a 'reconstitution stewardship programme'. To ensure the survivability and reliability of the defined reconstitution capabilities, nations would store components in separate locations in secured and hardened underground structures subject to special international inspection.

The defined period for reconstituting weapons capacity might be set initially at a few months. As nations adapt to and gain confidence in the new security arrangements, the defined time period might be extended further, within the framework of cooperative agreement and multinational monitoring. It is conceivable that the process of stretching the time period might continue, so that virtual deterrence, while never disappearing completely, would gradually fade and become progressivelylessimportantinsustainingnationalandinternational security.

Nuclear-reconstitution capacity would have to be transparent and subject to the most rigorous arrangements for monitoring and inspection. As verification systems became more rigorous, and nations gained confidence in the security of weaponless deterrence, the state of readiness for reconstitution could be eased. Every advance in inspection and mutual confidence-building would permit a lengthening of the world's nuclear fuse and consequently increase in the world's safety.[27]

The non-military foundations of security

The abolition of nuclear weapons does not mean that political disputes within and between states will cease. Armed conflicts remain widespread today, mostly within states, and they increasingly require international engagement and intervention by states and transnational organisations. Inter-state wars are infrequent and have been non-existent between major industrialised powers since 1945.[28] The old paradigm of industrialised inter-state war 'no longer exists', according to former senior British military commander Rupert Smith.[29] Yet the possibility of a war between major regional powers, such as India and Pakistan, and even their resort to nuclear weapons, cannot be ruled out. The risk of a regional nuclear exchange, however unlikely, is an important reason for integrating the regional NWS into the nuclear disarmament process.

Progress towards minimum deterrence and nuclear disarmament decreases the danger that conventional disputes will escalate to nuclear confrontation. The firewall between conventional war and the potential use of nuclear weapons remains tenuous, however, and has become more so with new security doctrines that expand the mission of nuclear weapons. Maintaining and reinforcing this separation is an important international security objective.

Vigorous efforts for the prevention and management of conventional military conflict are relevant to disarmament for multiple reasons. Conventional conflicts can be very destabilising and destructive, and may give rise to the consideration of nuclear weapons use. In some instances they may encourage states that have given up the bomb to revert to their earlier nuclear-weapons posture. States that engage in or fear the possibility of armed conflict will not feel secure in relinquishing their reliance on weapons of mass destruction.

The primary non-military strategy to promote peace and security is the development of cooperative security relations and effective mechanisms of conflict resolution. The safer states perceive their security environment to be, the less incentive they have to seek 'ultimate' weapons of mass annihilation. The objective of peace-building was well encapsulated in the mid-1950s by Karl W. Deutsch in the concept of a security community, which is a group of interacting states that do not plan to wage war against or aim weapons at each other.[30]

International relations research has produced solid empirical evidence that peace is most effectively promoted by a cluster of democratic practices, economic interdependence and commitment to international norms and institutions. These cornerstones of peace create virtuous circles of behaviour that reinforce each other and stem the outbreak and escalation of violent conflict. Democratic states do not fight each other, mutual interdependence in trade and finance produce common interests (sometimes involuntarily as in the China–US relationship) and international institutions establish common normative frameworks that guide cooperative behaviour and in some cases permit joint enforcement action. In a system characterised by these forms of behaviour states gain security not primarily through weapons capability but through the development of cooperative political and economic relations – through the advancement of democracy, economic prosperity, commercial interdependence and the defence of human rights. The best assurance of security in a world without nuclear weapons is the creation of more stable, cooperative political relations.

The strategies outlined above may be secondary considerations in drafting the blueprint for a non-nuclear world, but they are essential to the broader goal of reducing the likelihood of armed conflict and to that extent they help to make disarmament more likely. Realist theory argues that conflict prevention must precede disarmament, that states will not reduce their reliance on weapons until they feel more secure in their relations with other states. The policies identified here – the institutionalisation of democracy, economic interdependence and participation in multilateral institutions – do not provide simple answers to security dilemmas, but they are steps in the direction of increasing the prospect and sustainability of disarmament.

A Policy Agenda for Enhancing Security Without Nuclear Weapons

There are many policy options that would enable states to move in a step-by-step manner towards diminished reliance on nuclear weapons, further reductions in nuclear arsenals, stronger international verification and monitoring systems and the secure elimination of nuclear weapons.

The NWS should renew their negative security assurances, vowing never to use or threaten to use nuclear weapons against states that do not have such weapons. They should declare officially that the sole purpose of nuclear weapons is to deter the use or threat of use of such weapons by other states.

The United States and Russia should cooperate to negotiate additional nuclear arms-reduction agreements. They should establish a mutual process of dismantling nuclear weapons on reserve and eliminating classes of weapons, particularly short-range tactical arms. US–Russia cooperation is also needed to revitalise or replace the NATO–Russia Council, and to provide leadership in restructuring the Treaty on Conventional Forces in Europe (CFE).

The United States and China should pursue a range of confidence-building measures and mutual security assurances to increase the likelihood of cooperation in nuclear non-proliferation and disarmament. These would include bilateral discussions on space cooperation and missile defences, renewed military-to-military contacts and joint exercises and discussions of nuclear verification mechanisms for implementation of the test ban and a halt to the production of weapons-grade fissile material.

The United States should cooperate with states in Europe and East Asia to develop alternatives to extended nuclear deterrence-arrangements. This will require intensive consultations with government leaders and policy experts in these regions to evaluate regional security threats and define options for addressing security challenges without nuclear weapons.

The United States, Russia and other major states should intensify diplomatic engagement with India and Pakistan to achieve the goal of a more equitable global disarmament and non-proliferation regime. India should be welcomed to serve as a co-leader in global efforts to end reliance on nuclear weapons.

The United Nations and its member states should maintain and enforce sanctions on North Korea to prevent imports and exports of proliferation-sensitive and weapons-related technology and materials. Security Council sanctions should be combined with renewed offers of security assurances and the promise of normalised diplomatic and commercial relations, to encourage implementation of the 2005 Statement of Principles. Similar approaches are needed to dissuade Iran from developing nuclear weapons: effective implementation of Security Council sanctions, combined with inducements to encourage greater cooperation with the IAEA.

The United States and other major states should provide greater support for a comprehensive peace agreement in the Middle East structured along the lines of the widely accepted

Arab initiative. Such a settlement would be a necessary precondition for the development of a nuclear weapons-free zone in the region.

Donor states should provide a major boost in funding and institutional support for the IAEA. This would enable modernisation of the agency's infrastructure and research facilities, and the recruitment of a new generation of highly trained and well-paid verification specialists.

To encourage universal acceptance of the IAEA Additional Protocol, nuclear supplier states should make acceptance of the Additional Protocol a condition for the receipt of nuclear materials, services and technologies. NPT member states should support and seek universal adherence to a next generation 'Additional Protocol Plus' verification regime.

Negotiations should continue on the creation of multinational nuclear arrangements that can establish greater international control of the nuclear fuel cycle while guaranteeing universal access to nuclear fuel on a non-discriminatory basis. This might include the development of regulatory agencies to manage nuclear production in their region, cooperating fully with IAEA safeguards, to guarantee nuclear fuel for member states while assuring the peaceful character of production activities.

UN member states should maintain and enhance their compliance with Security Council Resolution 1540 (2004). Greater capacity-building and incentive efforts are needed to assist states in adopting laws and national enforcement measures against any forms of assistance to non-state actors seeking to develop weapons of mass destruction. The United States and other states should prioritise ratification of the Comprehensive Nuclear Test-Ban Treaty.

The United States should place limits on missile-defence deployments in the near term so as not to jeopardise reductions in strategic arms. Washington and Moscow should establish a multilateral planning process and cooperative research programme to develop shared defences for deployment after nuclear weapons have been abolished, as protection against potential nuclear break-out and cheating.

As they reduce nuclear weapons towards zero, the NWS should develop a planning process to define permissible states of readiness for reconstituting weapons and delivery systems after nuclear abolition. This would include agreement on the terms and conditions for preserving infrastructure maintenance programmes under rigorous international inspection.

GLOSSARY

ABACC	Brazilian–Argentine Agency for Accounting and Control of Nuclear Materials
ABM	Anti-ballistic missile
ACV	Armoured combat vehicle(s)
BMD	Ballistic-missile defense
CD	Conference on Disarmament
CFE	Conventional Forces in Europe
CIA	Central Intelligence Agency (US)
CSBM	Confidence- and security-building measure(s)
CSCE	Conference on Security and Co-operation in Europe
CTBT	Comprehensive Test-Ban Treaty, also referred to as the Comprehensive nuclear test Ban Treaty
CTBTO	Comprehensive Test-Ban Treaty Organisation
DPJ	Democratic Party of Japan
ENDC	Eighteen-Nation Committee on Disarmament
EU	European Union
FMCT	Fissile Material Cut-Off Treaty
GTRI	Global Threat Reduction Initiative
HEU	Highly enriched uranium (nuclear grade)
IAEA	International Atomic Energy Association
ICBM	Intercontinental ballistic missile(s)

IFOR	Implementation Force (NATO-led) in former Yugoslavia
IMS	International Monitoring System
INF	Intermediate-range nuclear forces
LEU	low-enriched uranium (non-weapons-grade)
MAD	Mutually assured destruction
MBFR	Mutual and Balanced Force Reduction(s)
MLF	Multilateral Force
MNA	Multilateral Nuclear Agreement(s)
NAM	Non-Aligned Movement
NATO	North Atlantic Treaty Organisation
NIE	National Intelligence Estimate (US)
NSG	Nuclear Suppliers Group
NPT	Treaty on the Non-Proliferation of Nuclear Weapons (or Nuclear Non-Proliferation Treaty)
NWS	Nuclear-weapons state(s)
NNWS	Non-nuclear weapons state(s)
PNI	Presidential Nuclear Initiatives
PSI	Proliferation Security Initiative
SDI	Strategic Defense Initiative
START	Strategic Arms Reduction Treaty
U-235	Fissile isotope of uranium
UN	United Nations
USSR	Union of Soviet Socialist Republics
VNA	Virtual nuclear arsenal(s)
WMD	Weapon(s) of mass destruction

NOTES

Preface

1   This is because of warhead counting rules that define a bomber as a single warhead, even when it may carry multiple independently targeted nuclear weapons. See Peter Baker, 'Arms Control May be Different Things on Paper and on the Ground', New York Times, 30 March 2010; also Pavel Podvig, 'Assessing START follow-on', *Bulletin of Atomic Scientists*, http://thebulletin.org/web-edition/columnists/pavel-podvig/assessing-start-follow.

Chapter One

1   United Nations General Assembly, *Resolutions Adopted on the Reports of the First Committee: Establishment of a Commission to Deal with the Problems Raised by the Discovery of Atomic Energy*, first. sess., 24 January 1946, available at http://www.un.org/documents/resga.htm.

2   McGeorge Bundy, *Danger and Survival: Choices about the Bomb in the First Fifty Years* (New York: Random House 1988), pp. 158–76.

3   Joseph Rotblat, a Nobel peace laureate, welcomed Gorbachev's speech as a revival of the old nuclear disarmament plans and the beginning of a new era in this regard. See Joseph Rotblat, 'Past Attempts to Abolish Nuclear Weapons', in Rotblat, Jack Steinberger and Bhalchandra Udgaonkar (eds), *A Nuclear-Weapon Free World: Desirable? Feasible?* (Boulder, CO: Westview Press 1993), pp. 17–32. See also Rebecca Johnson, 'Nuclear Disarmament Initiatives', paper prepared for the conference 'The NPT and a World Without Nuclear Weapons', organised by the Finnish Institute of International Affairs and the Kroc Institute for International Peace Studies at the University of Notre Dame, Helsinki, 22–24 October 2009.

4   Lawrence Freedman, 'I Exist, Therefore I Deter', *International Security*, vol. 13, no. 1, summer 1988, pp. 177–95.

5   Morton A. Kaplan, *System and Process in International Politics* (New York: John Wiley, 1957), pp. 50–2.

6   Michael Krepon, *Better Safe than Sorry: The Ironies of Living with the Bomb* (Stanford, CA: Stanford University Press, 2009), pp. 99–105.

7   See T.V. Paul, 'Complex Deterrence: An Introduction', in Paul, Patrick M. Morgan and James J. Wirtz (eds), *Complex Deterrence: Strategy in the Global Age* (Chicago, IL: University of Chicago Press, 2009).

8   For a critique of nuclear alarmism, see John Mueller, *Atomic Obsession: Nuclear Alarmism from Hiroshima to Al-Qaeda* (Oxford: Oxford University Press, 2009).

9   George P. Shultz, William J. Perry, Henry A. Kissinger and Sam Nunn, 'A World Free of Nuclear Weapons', *Wall Street Journal*, 4 January 2007.

10 Campbell Craig, 'American Power Preponderance and the Nuclear Revolution', *Review of International Studies*, vol. 35, no. 1, January 2009, pp. 27–44.

11 Barry Posen, 'Command of the Commons: The Military Foundation of U.S. Hegemony', *International Security*, vol. 28, no. 1, summer 2003, pp. 5–46.

12 Jonathan Schell, *The Gift of Time: The Case for Abolishing Nuclear Weapons Now* (New York: Metropolitan Books, 1998), p. 218.

13 Task Force on the United Nations, *American Interests and UN Reform* (Washington DC: United States Institute of Peace, 2005), p. 74.

14 Different forms and levels of deterrence are discussed in Tom Sauer, 'A Second Nuclear Revolution: From Nuclear Primacy to Post-Existential Deterrence', *Journal of Strategic Studies*, vol. 32, no. 5, October 2009, pp. 745–67.

15 In this context, we use the term 'virtual' in its literal meaning, 'existing in essence though not in actual fact'.

16 Scott D. Sagan, 'Shared Responsibilities for Nuclear Disarmament', *Daedalus*, fall 2009, pp. 157–8.

17 Johnson, 'Nuclear Disarmament Initiatives'.

18 See 'Arms Control Revisited: Non-proliferation and Denuclearization', report of the Warsaw Reflection Group, 20–21 November 2008 (Warsaw: Polish Institute of International Affairs, 2009); and T.V. Paul, 'Global Power Shift and the Proliferation of Nuclear Weapons', paper prepared for the conference 'The NPT and a World Without Nuclear Weapons', 2009, pp. 20–22.

19 William J. Perry, keynote address of the former Secretary of Defense at the conference 'Post-Cold War US Nuclear Strategy: A Search for Technical and Policy Common Ground', Committee on International Security and Arms Control, National Academy of Sciences, Washington DC, 11 August 2004, http://sites.nationalacademies. org/PGA/cisac/PGA_049763.

20 The Weapons of Mass Destruction Commission, *Weapons of Terror: Freeing the World of Nuclear, Biological, and Chemical Arms* (Stockholm: Weapons of Mass Destruction Commission, June 2006), p. 28, http://www. wmdcommission.org/files/Weapons_ of_Terror.pdf.

21 'Reinforcing the Global Nuclear Order for Peace and Prosperity: The Role of the IAEA to 2020 and Beyond', report prepared by an independent commission at the request of the Director General of

the International Atomic Energy Agency (IAEA), May 2008, p. 3, http://www.iaea.org/NewsCenter/News/PDF/2020report0508.pdf.

22 Rolf Mowatt-Larssen, 'Nuclear Security in Pakistan: Reducing the Risks of Nuclear Terrorism', *Arms Control Today*, vol. 39, no. 6, July–August 2009, p. 6.

23 Reagan's abolitionism has been documented by Paul Lettow, *Ronald Reagan and His Quest to Abolish Nuclear Weapons* (New York: Random House, 2005).

24 Quoted in Todd Fine, 'Using the Reagan Arms Control Legacy Correctly', *Bulletin of the Atomic Scientists*, 10 June 2009, available at http://www.thebulletin.org/web-edition/op-eds/.

25 Hans J. Morgenthau, 'Death in the Nuclear Age', *Commentary*, vol. 32, no. 3, September 1961, pp. 231–4.

26 Schell, 'The Abolition of Nuclear Arms: An Idea Whose Time Has Come', paper delivered as part of the International Security Studies Brady–Johnson Grand Strategy Lecture Series, Yale University, 25 March 2009.

Chapter Two

1 Lewis A. Dunn, 'The NPT: Assessing the Past, Building the Future', *Nonproliferation Review*, vol. 16, no. 2, July 2009, pp. 140–51.

2 B.I. Spinrad, 'A Projection of Nuclear Power and Associated Industry', in Bhupendra Jasani (ed.), *Nuclear Proliferation Problems* (Cambridge, MA: The MIT Press, 1974), pp. 25–40.

3 Susan Watkins, 'The Nuclear Non-Protestation Treaty', *New Left Review*, no. 54, November–December 2008, p. 21.

4 Harald Müller, 'Challenges Faced by the NPT', paper prepared for the conference 'The NPT and a World Without Nuclear Weapons', p. 7.

5 'Reinforcing the Global Nuclear Order for Peace and Prosperity: The Role of the IAEA to 2020 and Beyond', pp. 2–3.

6 Dinah Deckstein, Frank Dohmen and Cordula Meyer, 'Die Atom-Schlemperei', *Der Spiegel*, no. 42, 2009, pp. 118–21.

7 Sagan, 'Shared Responsibilities for Nuclear Disarmament', p. 160.

8 Oliver Meier, 'Nichtbereitung von Nuklearwaffen: Ist der Vertrag noch zu retten?', in Jochen Hippler et al. (eds), *Friedensgutachten* (Berlin: LIT Verlag, 2009), pp. 201–13.

9 'Documents: Resolutions Adopted at the NPT Extension Conference', *Arms Control Today*, vol. 25, no. 5, June 1995, p. 30.

10 The representatives of these two key countries – Alva Myrdal and Alfonso Garcia Robles – were even honoured with a the Nobel Peace Prize for their efforts to hold the nuclear-weapons states accountable, as did the IAEA and its Director General, Mohammed ElBaradei, in 2005.

11 'Reinforcing the Global Nuclear Order for Peace and Prosperity: The Role of the IAEA to 2020 and Beyond', report prepared by an independent commission at the request of the Director General of the International Atomic Energy Agency (IAEA), May 2008, p. 4, http://www.iaea.org/NewsCenter/News/PDF/2020report0508.pdf. 12

12 Mark Fitzpatrick, 'Nuclear Disarmament and Nonproliferation: Strengthening the Synergy', address to the IISS Global Strategic Review, Geneva, 12 September 2009.

13 United States Joint Chiefs of Staff, *Doctrine for Joint Theater Nuclear Operations*, Joint Pub 3-12.1, 9 February 1996, pp. III-6 and III-7, http://www.nukestrat.com/us/jcs/JCS_JP3-12-1_96.pdf.

14 Jacques Chirac, Speech to French Strategic Forces, Landivisiau, France, 19 January 2006, http://www.ambafrance-uk.org/Speech-by-M-Jacques-Chirac,6771.html

15 Schell, 'The Folly of Arms Control', *Foreign Affairs*, vol. 79, no. 5, September/October 2000, p. 32.

16 Remarks at the United States Institute of Peace, Hillary Rodham Clinton, Secretary of State, Renaissance Mayflower Hotel, Washington, DC, 21 October 2009.

17 'Reinforcing the Global Nuclear Order for Peace and Prosperity', pp. 4, 16.

18 David Holloway, *Stalin and the Bomb: The Soviet Union and Atomic Energy, 1939–1956* (New Haven, CT: Yale University Press, 1994), pp. 129, 132–3.

19 In Schell, *The Gift of Time: The Case for Abolishing Nuclear Weapons Now* pp. 58–9.

20 See Krepon, *Better Safe than Sorry*.

21 Morton Halperin wrote: 'The Bush administration decision to attack Iraq but not North Korea sent a clear message to Iran and other countries: only nuclear weapons deter the United States'. See Halperin, 'Promises and Priorities', in Halperin, Bruno Tertrais, Keth B. Payne, K Subrahmanyam, and Sagan, 'Forum: The Case for No First Use: An Exchange', *Survival*, vol. 51 no. 5, 2009, p. 22.

22 Sagan, 'Shared Responsibilities for Nuclear Disarmament', p. 158.

Chapter Three

1 'Reinforcing the Global Nuclear Order for Peace and Prosperity: The Role of the IAEA to 2020 and Beyond', p. 4, http://www.iaea.org/NewsCenter/News/PDF/2020report0508.pdf.

2 Joseph Cirincione, *Bomb Scare: The History and Future of Nuclear Weapons* (New York: Columbia University Press, 2007), pp. 43–4.

3 The counterargument is, of course, that the lower one goes in the general level of nuclear weapons, the more precious they become in relative terms and the more difficult it is to give them up.

4 Paul, *Power versus Prudence: Why Nations Forgo Nuclear Weapons* (Montréal: McGill–Queen's University Press, 2000), pp. 3–11.

5 Ariel E. Levite, 'Never Say Never Again: Nuclear Reversal Revisited', *International Security*, vol. 27, no. 3, Winter 2002–03, p. 68.

6 Harald Müller and Andreas Schmidt, 'The Little Known Story of De-Proliferation: Why States Give Up Nuclear Weapons Activities' (draft), paper presented at International Studies Association Convention, San Francisco, California, 26–29 March 2008,

http://www.allacademic.com//meta/p_mla_apa_research_citation/2/5/3/4/5/pages253459/p253459-1.php, forthcoming in William C. Potter (with Gaukhar Mukhatzhanova, ed), *Forecasting Nuclear Proliferation: The Role of Theory* (Stanford, CA: Stanford University Press, 2010).

7   When interpreting the results one has to remember that they are based on bivariate correlations which may hide more complex relationships between the variables.

8   Etel Solingen, *Nuclear Logics: Contrasting Paths in East Asia and the Middle East* (Princeton, NJ: Princeton University Press, 2007), pp. 14, 25.

9   Cirincione, *Bomb Scare*, pp. 45–6.

10   This is the general argument, supported by case studies, in Maria Rost Rublee, *Nonproliferation Norms: Why States Choose Nuclear Restraint* (Athens, GA: University of Georgia Press, 2009). Similar evidence on the positive impact of the normative environment can be seen in efforts to ban landmines and cluster munitions. These cases show, on the other hand, that those countries whose security is most directly affected by the ban tend to drag their feet and even oppose the ban.

11   George Perkovich, *India's Nuclear Bomb: The Impact on Global Proliferation*, updated edition (Berkeley, CA: University of California Press, 2002).

12   Müller and Schmidt, 'The Little Known Story of De-Proliferation', p. 36.

13   Mitchell Reiss, *Bridled Ambition: Why Countries Constrain Their Nuclear Capabilities* (Washington DC: The Woodrow Wilson Center Press, 1995), p. 332.

14   Perkovich, 'The Next Big Steps Required to Move toward Nuclear Disarmament', paper prepared for the conference, 'The NPT and a World without Nuclear Weapons', p. 1.

15   See David Cortright and George A. Lopez, *Sanctions and the Search for Security: Challenges to the UN Action* (Boulder, CO: Lynne Rienner Publishers, 2002).

16   Virginia I. Foran and Leonard S. Spector, 'The Application of Incentives to Nuclear Proliferation', in Cortright (ed), *The Price of Peace: Incentives and International Conflict Prevention* (Lanham, MD: Rowman & Littlefield Publishers, 1997), pp. 24–5.

17   See Gitty M. Amini, 'A Larger Role for Positive Sanctions in Cases of Compellance?', working paper no. 12, Center for International Relations, University of California, Los Angeles, CA, May 1997, pp. 27–8. In their study of 116 sanctions cases, Han Sorussen and Jongryn Mo also find that 'incentives increase the effectiveness of sanctions'. Sorussen and Mo, 'Sanctions and Incentives', paper delivered at the 1999 annual meeting of the American Political Science Association, Atlanta, Georgia, 2–5 September 1999, p. 2.

18   Reiss, *Bridled Ambition*, p. 326.

19   Leon V. Sigal, *Disarming Strangers: Nuclear Diplomacy with North Korea* (Princeton, NJ: Princeton University Press, 1998), p. 4.

20   Andrew Hurrell, 'An Emerging Security Community in South America', in Emanuel Adler and Michael Barnett (eds), *Security Communities* (Cambridge: Cambridge University Press, 1998), pp. 228–64; Nicholas J. Wheeler, 'Beyond Waltz's Nuclear World: More Trust May Be Better', *International Relations*, vol. 23, no. 3, 2009, pp. 434–42.

21   Reiss, *Bridled Ambition*, p. 66.

22   José Goldemberg, 'Looking Back: Lessons From the Denuclearization of

Brazil and Argentina', *Arms Control Today*, vol. 36, April 2006, http://www. armscontrol/print2023.

23 *Ibid.*

24 Reiss, *Bridled Ambition*, p. 68.

25 *Ibid.*, p. 28.

26 Paul Davis, 'Giving up the Bomb: Motivations and Incentives', International Commission on Nuclear Non-Proliferation and Disarmament, 2009.

27 Quoted in Reiss, *Bridled Ambition*, p. 32.

28 Rep. Tom Lantos, interview by Robert Siegel, *All Things Considered*, NPR, 30 January 2004.

29 Rost Rublee, *Nonproliferation Norms*, pp. 151–69.

30 US Department of State, 'Overview of State-Sponsored Terrorism', in *Patterns of Global Terrorism, 1996*, April 1997, http://www.state.gov/www/global/ terrorism/1996Report/overview.html.

31 Flynt Leverett, 'Why Libya Gave Up on the Bomb', *New York Times*, 23 January 2004, p. A23.

32 Thomas E. McNamara, 'Unilateral and Multilateral Strategies Against State Sponsors of Terror: A Case Study of Libya, 1979 to 2003', in Cortright and Lopez (eds), *Uniting Against Terror: Cooperative Nonmilitary Responses to the Global Terrorist Threat* (Cambridge, MA: MIT Press, 2007), pp. 83–122.

33 Paul, *Power versus Prudence*, pp. 117–20.

34 Reiss, *Bridled Ambition*, p. 3.

35 Foran and Spector, 'The Application of Incentives to Nuclear Proliferation', p. 40.

Chapter Four

1 Stephanie Cooke, *In Mortal Hands: A Cautionary History of the Nuclear Age* (New York: Bloomsbury, 2009).

2 Müller, 'Challenges Faced by the NPT', p. 16.

3 Morgenthau, *Politics Among Nations*, sixth edition (New York: Knopf, 1985), p. 439.

4 See 'Common Security: A Program of Disarmament', report of the International Commission on Disarmament and Security Issues, under the chairmanship of Olof Palme (Moscow: Progress Publishers, 1982). The concept of common security and the work of the Commission have been explored in Raimo Väyrynen (ed.), *Common Security* (London: Taylor & Francis, 1985); and in Cortright, 'Making the Case for Disarmament: An Analysis of the Palme and Canberra Commissions', in Unto Vesa (ed), *Global Commissions Assessed* (Helsinki: Finnish Edita Publishing Ltd., 2005), pp. 59–78.

5 Morgenthau, *Politics*, p. 107.

6 *Ibid.* p. 439.

7 Müller, 'Challenges Faced by the NPT', p. 2.

8 Perkovich, 'The Next Big Steps Required to Move toward Nuclear Disarmament', p. 2.

9 Alexander Wendt, 'The Anarchy Is What States Make of It: The Social Construction of Power Politics', *International Organization*, vol. 46, no. 2, spring 1992, pp. 420–2.

10 *Ibid.* See also Deborah Welch Larson, 'Crisis Prevention and the Austrian

State Treaty', *International Organization*, vol. 41, no. 1, winter 1987, pp. 27–60.

11   Charles E. Osgood, *An Alternative to War or Surrender* (Urbana, IL: University of Illinois Press, 1962).

12   Because the reductions were unilateral actions, they were not verifiable, and it is thus difficult to ascertain the total number of weapons withdrawn from service. The estimate of 17,000 is drawn from Nuclear Threat Initiative, 'Presidential Nuclear Initiatives: An Alternative Paradigm for Arms Control', issue brief, March 2004, http://www.nti.org/e_research/e3_41a.html.

13   Comments by Brent Scowcroft, Notre Dame International Security Program, Hesburgh Center for International Studies, University of Notre Dame, April 27 2009.

14   John Borawski, 'Accord at Stockholm', *Bulletin of The Atomic Scientists*, vol. 42,

no. 6, December 1986, p. 34, available at http://www.thebulletin.org.

15   'Gorbachev Hails the Stockholm Pact', *New York Times*, 25 September 1986, p. A6.

16   Wolgang Zellner, 'Can This Treaty be Saved? Breaking the Stalemate on Conventional Forces in Europe', *Arms Control Today*, vol. 39, no. 7, September 2009, http://www.armscontrol.org/act/2009_09/Zellner.

17   The phrase 'whole and free' is from a speech given by President George H.W. Bush in Germany in May 1989. For an analysis see William Forrest Harlow, 'And the Wall Came Tumbling Down: Bush's Rhetoric of Silence during German Reunification', in Martin J. Medhurst (ed.), *The Rhetorical Presidency of George H.W. Bush*, (College Station, TX: Texas A&M University Press, 2006), p. 40.

Chapter Five

1   United Nations Security Council (UNSC), *UN Security Council Resolution 1887* (2009), S/RES/1887, 24 September 2009, par. 9.

2   Jozef Goldblat, *Twenty Years of the Non-Proliferation Treaty: Implementation and Prospects* (Oslo: PRIO, 1990), pp. 37–40.

3   UNSC, *UN Security Council Resolution 984* (1995), S/RES/984, 11 April 1995, par. 1.

4   Michael Rühle, 'NATO and Extended Deterrence in a Multinuclear World', *Comparative Strategy*, vol. 28, no. 1, 2009, pp. 10–16.

5   Masa Takubo, 'The Role of Nuclear Weapons: Japan, the U.S., and "Sole

Purpose"', *Arms Control Today*, vol. 39, no. 9, November 2009, pp. 14–18.

6   'Reinforcing the Global Nuclear Order for Peace and Prosperity: The Role of the IAEA to 2020 and Beyond', prepared at the request of the Agency's director general, 2008, p. 16, http://www.iaea.org/NewsCenter/News/PDF/2020report0508.pdf.

7   Sagan, 'The Case for No First Use', *Survival*, vol. 51, no. 3, 2009, pps.168–69.

8   John A. Vasquez, 'The Deterrence Myth: Nuclear Weapons and the Prevention of Nuclear War', in Charles W. Kegley, Jr. (ed.), *The Long Postwar Peace: Contending Explanations and*

Projections (New York: HarperCollins, 1991), pp. 205–21.

9   John Lewis Gaddis, *The Long Peace: Inquiries into the History of the Cold War* (New York: Oxford University press, 1987), p. 230.

10 Ward Wilson, 'The Myth of Nuclear Deterrence', *Nonproliferation Review*, vol. 15, no. 3, November 2008, p. 422.

11 Perkovich, 'The Next Big Steps Required to Move toward Nuclear Disarmament', p. 7.

12 'Reinforcing the Global Nuclear Order for Peace and Prosperity', p. 17.

13 Sagan, 'Shared responsibilities for nuclear disarmament', p. 163.

14 Weapons of Mass Destruction Commission, *Weapons of Terror: Freeing the World of Nuclear, Biological, and Chemical Arms* (Stockholm: Weapons of Mass Destruction Commission, June 2006), pp. 72–3, http://www.wmdcommission.org/files/Weapons_of_Terror.pdf; Goldblat, *Twenty Years of the Non-Proliferation Treaty: Implementation and Prospects*, pp. 37–40.

15 Sagan, 'The Case for No First Use', pp. 163–82. This is not the first such debate. In the early 1980s, four leading statesmen issued a call for the United States to refrain from the first use of nuclear weapons, but Washington did not alter the official doctrine. See McGeorge Bundy, George Kennan, Robert McNamara and Gerard Smith, 'Nuclear Weapons and the Atlantic Alliance', *Foreign Affairs*, vol. 60, no. 4, Spring 1982, pp. 753–68.

16 The subsequent debate on Sagan's article conducted by Morton Halperin, Bruno Tertrais, Keith Payne and K. Subrahmanyam shows the 'no first use' pledge of nuclear weapons continues to divide national decision-makers and policy analysts. The key issues appear to be whether a no first use commitment would add anything significant to the existing restraints on the use of nuclear weapons felt by major powers and whether such pledges would be perceived as credible by the threshold countries. See Halperin, Tertrais, Payne and Subrahmanyam, 'No First Use: An Exchange', pp. 17–46.

17 Perkovich, 'The Next Big Steps Required to Move toward Nuclear Disarmament', p. 7.

18 *Ibid.*, p. 5.

19 *Ibid.*, p. 9.

20 Pavel Podvig, 'Assessing START follow-on', *Bulletin of Atomic Scientists*, http://thebulletin.org/web-edition/columnists/pavel-podvig/assessing-start-follow.

21 Oliver Meier, 'German Nuclear Stance Stirs Debate', *Arms Control Today*, vol. 39, no. 10, December 2009, pp. 30–2.

22 *Ibid.*,

23 Müller, 'Challenges Faced by the NPT', p. 20.

24 Andrew Scobell, 'Is There a Civil-Military Gap in China's Peaceful Rise?', *Parameters*, vol. 39, no. 2, July 2009, pp. 4–5.

25 European Council on Foreign Relations, Asia Centre, 'China Analysis: Is China A Reliable Partner in Non-Proliferation?', China Analysis no. 19, Sciences Po., August 2008, pp. 1–4, http://ecfr.3cdn.net/a77be9e83ad45d47d5_som6i2e4p.pdf.

26 See Bates Gill, *Rising Star: China's New Security Diplomacy* (Washington DC: Brookings Institution Press, 2007).

27 'National Security Strategy of the United States of America', US National Security Council brief (Washington, DC: US Government Printing Office, September 2002), p. 29; Patrick E.

Tyler, 'U.S. Strategy Plan Calls for Insuring No Rivals Develop A One-Superpower World', *New York Times*, 8 March 1992, http://www.nytimes.com/1992/03/08/world/us-strategy-plan-calls-for-insuring-no-rivals-develop.html?pagewanted=1.

Chapter Six

1 'India Launches First Nuclear Submarine', *Arms Control Today*, vol. 39, no. 7, September 2009, p. 41.

2 Pervez Hoobhoy, 'India's Nuclear Fizzle', *Dawn*, 2 September 2009, http://www.dawn.com/wps/wcm/connect/dawn-content-library/dawn/the-newspaper/editorial/indias-nuclear-fizzle-299

3 *Congressional Quarterly*, 16 May 1992, p. 1352.

4 Müller, 'Challenges Faced by the NPT', p. 14.

5 Sigal, 'Negotiating with the North', *Bulletin of the Atomic Scientists*, vol. 59, no. 6, November–December 2003, p. 20; Sigal, *Disarming Strangers: Nuclear Diplomacy with North Korea*.

6 Quoted in Sigal, 'Averting a Train Wreck with North Korea', *Arms Control Today*, vol. 28, no. 8, November–December 1998, p. 14.

7 Quoted in Sigal, 'Negotiating with the North', p. 20.

8 Scott Snyder, 'North Korea's Nuclear Program: The Role of Incentives in Preventing Deadly Conflict', in Cortright (ed), *The Price of Peace: Incentives and International Conflict Prevention* (Lanham, MD.: Rowman & Littlefield Publishers, 1997), p. 69.

9 See Sigal, 'Averting a Train Wreck with North Korea', p. 12.

28 Perkovich, 'The Next Big Steps Required to Move toward Nuclear Disarmament', p. 10.

29 Robert Rhodes James, ed., *Winston S. Churchill: His Complete Speeches, 1897–1963, vol. VI: 1935–1942* (London, Chelsea House, 1974), p.8625.

10 Quoted in Sigal, 'Negotiating with the North', p. 21.

11 Victor Cha, 'Up Close and Personal, Here's What I Learned', *Washington Post*, 14 June 2009, http://www.washingtonpost.com/wp-dyn/content/article/2009/06/12/AR2009061202685.html.

12 Pam Benson, 'Iran Resumes Nuclear Weapons Work, US Report Expected to Say', CNN, 12 February 2010, http://www.cnn.com/2010/POLITICS/02/11/us.iran.nuclear/index.html.

13 IAEA Board of Governors, 'Implementation of the NPT Safeguards Agreement and Relevant Provisions of Security Council Resolutions 1737 (2006) and 1747 (2007) in the Islamic Republic of Iran: Report of the Director General', GOV/2007/58, 15 November 2007, par. 43, http://www.iaea.org/Publications/Documents/Board/2007/gov2007-58.pdf; Ariane Bernard and Elaine Sciolino, 'Nuclear Agency Says Iran Has Improved Cooperation', *New York Times*, 23 November 2007, p. A14.

14 Mohamed ElBaradei, Introductory Statement to the Board of Governors by the IAEA Director General, Vienna, Austria, 22 November 2007, http://www.iaea.org/NewsCenter/Statements/2007/ebsp2007n019.html.

15 Peter Crail, 'IAEA Rebukes Iran over Secret Facility', *Arms Control Today*, vol. 39, no. 7, September 2009, p. 29.

16 IAEA Board of Governors, 'Implementation of the NPT Safeguards Agreement and Relevant Provisions of Security Council Resolutions 1737 (2006), 1747 (2007), 1803 (2008), and 1835 (2008) in the Islamic Republic of Iran: Report of the Director General', paras. 12 and 17, and 31–2.

17 'Bush Authorizes New Covert Action against Iran', ABC News. 22 May 2007, http://blogs.abcnews.com/theblotter/2007/05/bush_authorizes.html.

18 Seymour M. Hersh, 'Preparing the Battlefield: The Bush Administration Steps Up its Secret Moves Against Iran', *The New Yorker*, 7 July 2008, http://www.newyorker.com/reporting/2008/07/07/080707fa_fact_hersh.

19 'Sanctions Would Just Hit the People, Says Iran's Opposition Leader', TopNews.in, 28 September 2009, http://www.topnews.in/people/mirhossein-moussavi .

20 Perkovich and Goldschmidt, 'Establishing the Right Precedent in Supplying Fuel to Iran', proliferation analysis, Carnegie Endowment for International Peace, 7 October 2009, http://www.carnegieendowment.org/publications/index.cfm?fa=view&id=23970.

21 Aluf Benn, 'Israel Will Agree to Nuclear Free Zone to Begin Two Years after Signing a Regional Peace Agreement' (in Hebrew), *Ha'aretz*, 21 February 1995, p. 1.

22 Avner Cohen, *Israel and the Bomb* (New York: Columbia University Press, 1998), p. 10.

23 Müller, 'Challenges Faced by the NPT', p. 13.

24 Morgenthau, *Politics Among Nations*, sixth edition (New York: Knopf, 1985), p. 78.

Chapter Seven

1 'Reinforcing the Global Nuclear Order for Peace and Prosperity: The Role of the IAEA to 2020 and Beyond', p. 21, http://www.iaea.org/NewsCenter/News/PDF/2020report0508.pdf.

2 Goldschmidt, 'Exposing Nuclear Non-compliance', *Survival*, vol. 51, no. 1, 2009, pp. 143–64. The author served previously as Deputy Director General of the IAEA.

3 *Ibid.*, pp. 9–10. See also Goldblat, 'Amending the Non-Proliferation Regime', *Disarmament Forum*, no. 1–2, 2009, pp. 37–9 and Paul Meyer, 'Saving the NPT: Time to Renew Treaty Commitments', *Nonproliferation Review*, vol. 16, no. 3, 2009, pp. 467–8.

4 'Reinforcing the Global Nuclear Order for Peace and Prosperity', p. 18.

5 James M. Acton, 'The Problem with Nuclear Mind Reading', *Survival*, vol. 51, no. 1, February–March 2009, pp. 119–42.

6 For a detailed analysis of the role of the Security Council in disarmament issues, see United Nations Security Council, 'The Security Council's Role in Disarmament and Arms Control: Nuclear Weapons, Non-Proliferation and Other Weapons of

Mass Destruction', no. 2, New York, 1 September 2009.

7   Müller, 'Was wäre, wenn? Wie kann sich die internationale Gemeinschaft in einer kernwaffenfreie Welt gegen Regelbrecher durchsetzen?', Hessische Stiftung Friedens- und Konfliktforschung Report, 4/2009, Frankfurt am Main, pp. 10–13.

8   United Nations Security Council, Note by the President of the Security Council, S/23500, 31 January 1992.

9   Goldschmidt, 'Safeguards Noncompliance: A Challenge for the IAEA and the UN Security Council', Arms Control Today, vol. 40, no. 1, January–February 2010, 25–6.

10 'Reinforcing the Global Nuclear Order for Peace and Prosperity', pp. vii–viii, pp. 28–9.

11 'IAEA Budget Gets Modest Boost', Arms Control Today, vol. 39, no. 7, September 2009, p. 34.

12 Ollie Heinonen, remarks at the conference, 'The NPT and a World Without Nuclear Weapons', organised by the Finnish Institute of International Affairs and the Kroc Institute for International Peace Studies at the University of Notre Dame, Helsinki, 22–24 October 2009.

13 Perkovich and James M. Acton, 'Abolishing Nuclear Weapons', Adelphi Paper 396 (London: Routledge for the IISS, 2008), pp. 73–8.

14 Perkovich, 'The Next Big Steps Required to Move toward Nuclear Disarmament', p. 4.

15 'Reinforcing the Global Nuclear Order for Peace and Prosperity', p. 16.

16 Sagan, 'Shared Responsibilities for Nuclear Disarmament', p. 160.

17 'Uranium Enrichment', Q&A, BBC News, 1 September 2006, http://news.bbc.co.uk/ 2/hi/middle_east/5278806.stm.

18 'Reinforcing the Global Nuclear Order for Peace and Prosperity', p. 10.

19 UNSC, UN Security Council Resolution 1887 (2009), S/RES/1887, 24 September 2009, par. 14.

20 Mohamed ElBaradei, 'Towards a Safer World', The Economist, 16 October 2003, http://www.iaea.org/NewsCenter/Statements/2003/ebTE20031016.html.

21 Javier Solana, 'Strengthening Disarmament and the Non-Proliferation Regime', in Hannes Swaboda and Jan Marinus Wiersma (eds), Peace and Disarmament: A World Without Nuclear Weapons? (Brussels: The Socialist Group in the European Parliament, 2009), pp. 29–33.

22 'Opening Remarks of Thomas H. Kean and Lee H. Hamilton, Chair and Vice Chair of the 9/11 Public Discourse Project', report on Status of 9/11 Commission Recommendations, Part III: Foreign Policy, Public Diplomacy and Non-Proliferation, 14 November 2005, Washington, DC, p. 3, http://www.9-11pdp.org/press/2005-11-14_remarks.pdf.

23 Defense Threat Reduction Agency, 'Cooperative Threat Reduction Annual Report to Congress Fiscal Year 2010', 31 December 2008, p. 2, available at http://www.dtra.mil.

24 United States Department of Energy, 'U.S. and Russia Sign Plan for Russian Plutonium Disposition', press release, 19 November 2007, http://www.npec-web.org/Essays/20080612-Zarate-Sokolsky-UsRussiaOverview.pdf.

25 National Nuclear Security Administration, 'NNSA Announces Equivalent of More than 15,000 Nuclear Weapons of Russian HEU Eliminated', press release, 23 September 2009, http://nnsa.energy.gov/news/2592.htm.

26 Cirincione, *Bomb Scare*, pp. 141–2.

27 National Nuclear Security Administration, 'GTRI: Reducing Nuclear Threats', fact sheet, January 2009, http://www.nnsa.energy.gov/news/2330.htm.

28 Center for Defense Information, 'The Global Threat Reduction Initiative's First Two Years', 6 September 2006, http://www.cdi.org/program/document.cfm?DocumentID=3650; see also 'Fiscal Year 2010 Budget Tables for the National Nuclear Security Administration', US Department of Energy, p. 27, http://nnsa.energy.gov/news/documents/NNSA_Budget_Tables_FY2010(2).pdf.

29 'Fiscal Year 2010 Budget Tables for the National Nuclear Security Administration', US Department of Energy, p. 28.

30 Proliferation Security Initiative Participants website, US Department of State, http://www.state.gov/t/isn/c27732.htm.

31 Condoleezza Rice, 'Remarks on the Second Anniversary of the Proliferation Security Initiative', US Department of State, Washington, DC, 31 May 2005, http://merln.ndu.edu/archivepdf/wmd/State/46951.pdf.

32 Tony Foley, 'Opening Remarks, PSI Operational Experts Group Meeting', Proliferation Security Initiative Meeting, Sopot, Poland, 22 June 2009, pp. 6–7, http://dtirp.dtra.mil/TIC/treatyinfo/psi/psi_remarks.pdf.

33 US Department of State, Proliferation Security Initiative Ship Boarding Agreements website, http://www.state.gov/t/isn/c27733.htm. These states include Bahamas, Belize, Croatia, Cyprus, Liberia, Malta, Marshall Islands, Mongolia and Panama; see also Joel A. Doolin, 'The Proliferation Security Initiative: Cornerstone of a New International Norm', *Naval War College Review*, vol. 59, no. 2, spring 2006, pp. 29–57.

34 United Nations Security Council, *UN Security Council Resolution 1874 (2009) [Non-proliferation/Democratic People's Republic of Korea]*, S/RES/1874, 12 June 2009, p. 3, paras 11–12.

35 Simeon Kerr and Harvey Morris, 'N Korean Arms for Iran Seized by UAE', *Financial Times*, 28 August 2009, http://www.ft.com/cms/s/0/1cc52dcc-93f6-11de-9c57-00144feabdc0.html?nclick_check=1; see also Richard Lloyd Perry, 'Thai Police Seize North Korean Aircraft Carrying 40 Tons of Heavy Weapons', *The Times*, 13 December 2009, http://www.timesonline.co.uk/tol/news/world/asia/article6954868.ece.

36 Amitai Etzioni, 'Tomorrow's Institution Today: The Promise of the Proliferation Security Initiative', *Foreign Affairs*, vol. 88, no. 3, May/June 2009, pp. 7–11.

37 Kaegan McGratth, 'Verifiability, Reliability, and National Security: The Case for U.S. Ratification of the CTBT', *Nonproliferation Review*, vol. 16, no. 3, 2009, pp. 407–27.

38 See David Albright and Corey Gay, 'A flash from the past', *Bulletin of the Atomic Scientists*, vol. 53, no. 6 (1997), p. 16. For a comprehensive review of the decades-long controversy over whether a nuclear test occurred, see National Security Archive Electronic Briefing Book No. 190 at http://www.gwu.edu/~nsarchiv/NSAEBB/NSAEBB190/index.htm.

39 Daryl G. Kimball, 'For a Safer America: The Case for the Comprehensive Test Ban Treaty', fact sheet, Arms Control Association, Washington, DC, October 2009, http://www.armscontrol.org/factsheets/CaseStatement.

40 Sam Nunn, 'The Mountaintop: A World Without Nuclear Weapons', remarks at the International Conference on Nuclear Disarmament, Oslo, Norway, 27 February 2008, http://www.nti.org/c_press/speech_Nunn_Oslo022708.pdf.

Chapter Eight

1   Kissinger, 'Strategy and the Atlantic Alliance', *Survival*, vol. 24, no. 5, September 1982, p. 197.
2   Council on Foreign Relations, *US Nuclear Weapons Policy*, Independent Task Force Report No. 62 (New York: Council on Foreign Relations, 2009), p. 45.
3   James E. Goodby and Sidney D. Drell, *A World Without Nuclear Weapons: End-State Issues* (Palo Alto, CA: Stanford University Press, 2009), p. 23.
4   David Holloway, 'Further Reductions in Nuclear Forces', in George P. Shultz et al. (eds), *Reykjavik Revisited*, (Stanford, CA: Hoover Press, 2008).
5   Perkovich, 'The Next Big Steps Required to Move toward Nuclear Disarmament', p. 2.
6   *Ibid.*, p. 2.
7   See Sagan, 'Shared Responsibilities for Nuclear Disarmament', p. 165.
8   Perkovich, 'The Next Big Steps Required to Move Toward Nuclear Disarmament', p. 11.
9   Michael Mazarr (ed), *Nuclear Weapons in a Transformed World* (New York: St Martin's Press, 1997), p. 4.
10 Stansfield Turner, *Caging the Genies: A Workable Solution for Nuclear, Chemical, and Biological Weapons* (Boulder, CO: Westview Press, 1999), p. 82.
11 *Ibid.*, p. 85.
12 Mazarr (ed), *Nuclear Weapons in a Transformed World*, pp. 371–72.
13 *Ibid.*, p. 14.
14 *Ibid.*, p. 6.
15 Väyrynen, 'Controversies Over Missile Defense in Europe', *Working Papers 2009*, No. 59 (Helsinki: The Finnish Institute of International Affairs, 2009).
16 Schell, *The Seventh Decade: The New Shape of Nuclear Danger* (New York: Metropolitan Books, 2007), p. 190.
17 *Ibid.*, pp. 193–5.
18 This quote and all Reagan and Gorbachev quotes from the Reykjavík summit in this and the following paragraph are drawn from the recounting of the official transcript in Schell, *The Seventh Decade*, pp. 190–96.
19 Perkovich, 'The Next Big Steps Required to Move toward Nuclear Disarmament', p. 14.
20 Jonathan Schell, *The Abolition* (New York: Alfred A. Knopf, 1984), p. 153.
21 Schell, 'The Abolition of Nuclear Arms: An Idea Whose Time Has Come', paper delivered as part of the International Security Studies Brady-Johnson Grand Strategy Lecture Series, Yale University, 25 March 2009.
22 Levite, 'Never Say Never Again: Nuclear Reversal Revisited', *International Security*, vol. 27, no. 3, Winter 2002–03, p. 72.
23 *Ibid.*, p. 75.
24 Goodby and Drell, *A World Without Nuclear Weapons: End-State Issues*, p. 6.
25 *Ibid.*, p. 13.
26 *Ibid.*, p. 27.

27 Schell, *The Abolition* (New York: Alfred A. Knopf, 1984), p. 139.

28 Väyrynen (ed), *The Waning of Major War: Theories and Debates* (London: Routledge, 2006).

29 Rupert Smith, *The Utility of Force: The Art of War in the Modern World* (London: Penguin Books, 2006), pp. 1–2.

30 See Karl W. Deutsch et al., *Political Community at the North Atlantic Level* (Princeton, NJ: Princeton University Press , 1954); Emanuel Adler and Patrick Morgan (eds), *Security Communities* (Cambridge: Cambridge University Press, 2000).

⟮IISS ADELPHI BOOKS

ADELPHI 409

Climate Conflict: How global warming threatens security and what to do about it

Jeffrey Mazo

ISBN 978-0-415-59118-8

ADELPHI 408

Building Asia's Security

Nick Bisley

ISBN 978-0-415-58266-7

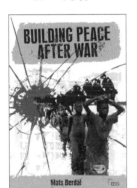

ADELPHI 407

Building Peace After War

Mats Berdal

ISBN 978-0-415-47436-8

ADELPHI 406

Transforming Pakistan: Ways out of instability

Hilary Synnott

ISBN 978-0-41556-260-7

Adelphi books are published eight times a year by Routledge Journals, an imprint of Taylor & Francis, 4 Park Square, Milton Park, Abingdon, Oxfordshire OX14 4RN, UK.

A subscription to the institution print edition, ISSN 0567-932X, includes free access for any number of concurrent users across a local area network to the online edition, ISSN 1478-5145.

2010 Annual Adelphi Subscription Rates			
Institution	£457	$803 USD	€673
Individual	£230	$391 USD	€312
Online only	£433	$763 USD	€640

Dollar rates apply to subscribers outside Europe. Euro rates apply to all subscribers in Europe except the UK and the Republic of Ireland where the pound sterling price applies. All subscriptions are payable in advance and all rates include postage. Journals are sent by air to the USA, Canada, Mexico, India, Japan and Australasia. Subscriptions are entered on an annual basis, i.e. January to December. Payment may be made by sterling cheque, dollar cheque, international money order, National Giro, or credit card (Amex, Visa, Mastercard).

For more information, visit our website: **http://www.informaworld.com/ adelphipapers.**

For a complete and up-to-date guide to Taylor & Francis journals and books publishing programmes, and details of advertising in our journals, visit our website: **http://www.informaworld.com.**

Ordering information:
USA/Canada: Taylor & Francis Inc., Journals Department, 325 Chestnut Street, 8th Floor, Philadelphia, PA 19106, USA. **UK/Europe/Rest of World:** Routledge Journals, T&F Customer Services, T&F Informa UK Ltd., Sheepen Place, Colchester, Essex, CO3 3LP, UK.

Advertising enquiries to:
USA/Canada: The Advertising Manager, Taylor & Francis Inc., 325 Chestnut Street, 8th Floor, Philadelphia, PA 19106, USA. Tel: +1 (800) 354 1420. Fax: +1 (215) 625 2940.

UK/Europe/Rest of World: The Advertising Manager, Routledge Journals, Taylor & Francis, 4 Park Square, Milton Park, Abingdon, Oxfordshire OX14 4RN, UK. Tel: +44 (0) 20 7017 6000. Fax: +44 (0) 20 7017 6336.

The print edition of this journal is printed on ANSI conforming acid-free paper by Bell & Bain, Glasgow, UK.

0567-932X(2009)49:7;1-U